Patents for Business

Patents for Business

The Manager's Guide to Scope, Strategy, and Due Diligence

M. Henry Heines

PRAEGER

Westport, Connecticut
London

Library of Congress Cataloging-in-Publication Data

Heines, M. Henry, 1945–
    Patents for business : the manager's guide to scope, strategy, and due
diligence / M. Henry Heines.
        p. cm.
    Includes bibliographical references and index.
    ISBN 0–275–99337–X (alk. paper)
    1. Patent laws and legislation—United States—Popular works.
2. Patents—United States—Popular works.   I. Title.
KF3114.6.H395   2007
346.7304'86—dc22   2006038653

British Library Cataloguing in Publication Data is available.

Library of Congress Catalog Card Number: 2006038653
ISBN-10: 0–275–99337–X
ISBN-13: 978–0–275–99337–5

First published in 2007

Praeger Publishers, 88 Post Road West, Westport, CT 06881
An imprint of Greenwood Publishing Group, Inc.
www.praeger.com

Printed in the United States of America

∞™

The paper used in this book complies with the
Permanent Paper Standard issued by the National
Information Standards Organization (Z39.48–1984).

10 9 8 7 6 5 4 3 2 1

Contents

List of Figures

Preface

Anyone with the most rudimentary Internet searching skills can find an enormous selection and variety of publications on patents and intellectual property in general. Much of the variety is in the depth and level of sophistication of the subject matter and in the target readership. Books for professional patent practitioners differ from books for inventors seeking to proceed without an attorney, and both will differ further from intellectual property survey books for law students or from reference books for scientists, engineers, or managers who simply wish to supplement their technical libraries with a basic book on patents. The available publications range from pamphlets to multivolume treatises, and those that are directed to one readership sector are often inappropriate for, or of little practical use to, the other sectors. There are some in the business community who believe that patent matters are best left entirely to patent attorneys, given the specialized nature of patent law and the ever-changing nature of patent laws, regulations, and procedures worldwide, and who therefore shun any involvement in patent-related decisions. The services of a skilled patent attorney are indeed essential to successful patenting, but business interests are not served by using the patent attorney as the sole resource.

My interest in writing for the business professional arises from my observations of the ever-increasing importance of patenting strategies in business operations and in establishing a defensible foothold in the industrial marketplace. Judging from settlements and verdicts over the past few years, the revenue that a single patent or a portfolio of related patents can provide, and likewise the cost of a patent to an infringer, has reached well into the hundreds of millions of dollars.

Also increasing are the number of patent-holding entities that can generate revenue, in some cases of this magnitude, without manufacturing or selling a single product. Regardless of the nature of one's business, a strong patent portfolio gives a business entity a value that far exceeds the entity's net book worth. A strong patent portfolio also provides leverage and a strong bargaining position in negotiating joint ventures and strategic alliances, generating licensing revenue, and attracting investors. These transactions and the decisions that control and direct them are made by management, not patent attorneys. The project manager, group leader, or R&D director may have a different degree or type of involvement than a corporate officer or a member of the board of directors, but patents enter into management decisions at many levels, and any manager may have to answer to the stockholders and to upper management when wrong decisions are made. Patents are thus a major corporate asset, and knowledge of how patent rights are created, managed, and exploited to maximum effect is a valuable management skill.

This book originated as an attempt to prepare managers for intellectual property due diligence, since due diligence is a critical step in many corporate transactions and often finds the manager answering probing questions from a skilled patent professional, questions that the manager is often unprepared for. As this book was being written, however, its scope expanded to encompass patent questions in general that arise in the course of doing business, and to educate clients in matters that patent attorneys would like their clients to be sensitive to in the creation of a truly collaborative attorney-client working relationship and in the securement of a strong yet cost-effective patent position for the client. This book therefore is an attempt to provide a sophisticated and thorough, yet accessible, resource that the manager will use again and again as patent matters arise, whether during due diligence or in the manager's routine decision-making duties, to place the corporation on a solid footing in patent matters.

Chapter 1

Being Prepared for
Due Diligence

With the proliferation of alliances, acquisitions, investments, and deals and fund-raising activities in general that occur in today's technology climate, any technology business entity has a high likelihood of enduring at least one due diligence review. Due diligence typically involves exposing internal and confidential information to outside counsel who is otherwise unfamiliar with the company's operations or technology and yet must review the company's entire intellectual property landscape and make recommendations within a limited period of time. Information revealed in the review can be the controlling factor in the reviewer's decision as to whether or not to recommend that the transaction or investment go forward. Because of the pivotal role of due diligence in these matters, any business entity will benefit from an understanding of due diligence and the issues that it can reveal. This chapter will illustrate how due diligence impacts most if not all of the aspects of intellectual property.

WHAT IS DUE DILIGENCE?

The term "due diligence" originated in Section 11(b)(3) of the Securities Act of 1933, which was enacted to protect the public interest when equities in a company were sold in public offerings. In certain offerings, the value of the equities dropped precipitously soon after the sales took place. The devaluation resulted from unfavorable facts about the company that had not surfaced until after the offering had been made, and in many cases this resulted in disastrous consequences to the buyers. Since the company was rarely in a position to compensate the buyers for their losses, the buyers' only recourse was to file claims against the brokers and dealers who coordinated the sale. The Securities Act provided a statutory basis for these claims by establishing a standard of behavior for brokers and dealers, requiring that they conduct an investigation into the company before an offering is made and that they exercise "due diligence" in the investigation, i.e., that they conduct the investigation in a manner reasonably calculated to uncover all of the facts an investor might consider important in deciding whether or not to purchase the equities. If the brokers and dealers could show that they met this standard, the Securities Act provided them with a defense against the investors' claims.

The recognition of the need to know all of the relevant facts before closing a business transaction has expanded greatly since 1933, as has the potential liability for anyone dealing in equities. As a result, due diligence is now a recognized standard for investigations preceding almost any transaction that involves the sale or transfer of all or part of a commercial entity or of particular commercial assets, regardless of whether the transferor is an individual or a business entity. A due diligence review commonly precedes any transaction in which the value of the asset being sold or the interest being acquired is a factor of any significance in the transaction, or where there is any potential for liability arising from the transfer. Indeed, any transaction in which the interests of investors, ranging all the way from individuals to multinational conglomerates and including funds and partnerships as well as corporations, may be affected can be expected to undergo due diligence.

The investigation is performed after the parties have agreed in principle to the transaction but before the transaction closes and the parties are fully obligated. If the investigation produces a report that is entirely favorable, the transaction may go forward as planned. If the investigation reveals that the value of the transaction is far below what was originally contemplated, that there are significant obstacles to obtaining the full value of the transaction, or that certain risks are present that the acquiring party is unwilling to assume, the transaction may be canceled entirely. Alternatively, the report may convince the two parties to the transaction to agree to modified terms. For example, a low valuation of the assets and a high magnitude of risk can be factored into the purchase price. Risks can also be allocated in accordance with the findings: a particular risk can be assumed in exchange for a concession from the party with which the risk originated; one side can be persuaded to assume risks that are too costly or difficult for the other to assume; or certain assets can be selected for inclusion in the transaction and others excluded.

When properly done, the due diligence review is conducted by an independent outside counsel who has no interest in the transaction or in any of the parties. The outside counsel is commonly engaged, and paid, by the investigator, i.e., the party that will be injured by any misrepresentations made or unfavorable facts discovered during the course of the transaction. The entity or asset being investigated is commonly termed the "target," and targets can vary as widely as the transactions themselves. In a stock offering, the target is the company whose shares are being offered and the investigator is the potential buyer or the buyer's representative. In a merger of two corporations, either corporation can be the target, and in many cases, each acts as an investigator and conducts a due diligence review of the other. In an acquisition of one business entity by another and often larger business entity, the acquired entity is the target and the acquiring entity is the investigator. In a joint venture, either partner of the venture can be a target of an investigation by the other. When a venture capitalist seeks to make an investment in a startup or any company seeking capital, the venture capitalist is the investigator and the startup or company is the target. Due diligence investigations can also be conducted by lenders before making a loan, with the borrower being the target. In any acquisition of rights to intellectual property, either by option, license, or purchase, the target is the intellectual property asset(s) to which rights are being acquired, and the investigator is the acquiring party.

THE SCOPE OF DUE DILIGENCE

The purposes of a due diligence review are to assess the value of the asset to be transferred and to identify and evaluate any risks involved in the transaction. The documents that will be reviewed and the matters that will be explored by the investigator will depend on the transaction. The scope of the review can include such diverse matters as the financial assets of the target, regulatory concerns (for example, whether the relevant compliances have been met and clearances obtained), political factors, infrastructure factors, labor factors, taxation factors, general litigation risks, and intellectual property.

Intellectual property due diligence occurs in any transaction involving rights to technology, and may constitute the entire investigation or a large part of it. The issues in intellectual property due diligence generally fall within two categories:

1. Does the target have the legal right to practice the technology and will those rights remain intact if the transaction is completed? Among the questions relevant to this issue are whether there any patent rights held by others that would limit or interfere with the target's free ability, or the ability of any other party to the transaction, to continue to practice the technology after the transfer has been made.

2. Does the target have the legal means to exclude competitors from practicing the technology? In particular, is the technology covered by enforceable patent rights that are exclusively owned or held by the target; does the target have the full right to assert the patents over infringers; and will this right be transferred intact when the transaction takes place?

DUE DILIGENCE VERSUS WARRANTIES

Every transaction involving the transfer or acquisition of assets or rights will contain warranties, and one may well wonder whether these warranties render due diligence reviews redundant. Certainly in intellectual property due diligence, all of the concerns listed above can be covered by warranties or indemnities. Why then should one invest in the expense of a due diligence review when the warranties or indemnities in the contract can be specifically worded to cover the same issues?

Warranties and indemnities are indeed useful for a variety of matters, but they are generally of limited duration and often of limited amount. For this reason, warranties and indemnities are inappropriate for many intellectual property matters. Furthermore, a warranty or indemnity clause typically contains cumbersome requirements for the party seeking to invoke the clause. The clause may, for example, require advance notice to the warrantor that a claim will be made, or may apply only when the misrepresentation or loss is "material," a standard that is often difficult to define and to show as having been met. In some cases, the clause applies only when the warrantor had "reasonable knowledge" of the problem that caused the loss, which likewise can be difficult to define and to show as having been met. Even if all requirements for a claim under a warranty are met, the warranty may not fully compensate the injured party, particularly if the loss that was suffered is not one that can be adequately compensated for by money. And even if money were sufficient, the warrantor might not have sufficient assets to meet the claim.

Certain warranties and indemnities will necessarily be included in the transaction regardless of whether a due diligence review precedes the closing, since there will be various matters that are unreasonable or uneconomical for the investigator to check. For example, the contract will typically contain a warranty by the target that the information the target supplies to the investigator is complete and accurate. Nevertheless, for the bulk of the intellectual property issues that will determine the risks and the value of transaction, it is far more expedient, efficient, and effective to investigate these issues in a due diligence review and identify them before they become losses.

IMPROVING ONE'S CHANCES FOR SUCCESSFUL INTELLECTUAL PROPERTY DUE DILIGENCE

Almost any company's long-range business goals include transactions, large or small, in which intellectual property rights are a key component, and the chances that the transaction will succeed to the company's benefit can be improved if the company maintains an awareness of possible due diligence issues from the start of its operations. Awareness and preparation will expedite the review and avoid or minimize oversights, omissions, and discoveries that might prompt the other party to devalue the transaction or withdraw from it entirely. The following are some of the most common questions raised in intellectual property due diligence.

Right to Use

1. Have freedom-to-operate searches been performed?
2. Have any patents to others been found, in freedom-to-operate searches or otherwise, that appear to cover any part of the

technology of interest or similar (and possibly overlapping) technologies? If so, have legal analyses of these patents been obtained and legally supported opinions been rendered to determine whether infringement exists and whether the patents are valid?

3. Have any threats of enforcement of patent rights or suggestions of threats been received from outside patent holders? Suggestions of threats might include seemingly benign notices from patent holders of the existence or imminent issuance of a patent, whether the notice includes an offer for license or sale or a demand for royalties or for cessation of operations or sales. If such threats or suggestions have been received, how have they been resolved?

4. In small-scale transactions, the questions in items 1, 2, and 3 above will be limited to U.S. patents and commercial operations, whereas in transactions involving operations abroad and multinational corporations, the same questions will apply to patents, operations, and threats in jurisdictions outside the United States.

5. If the right to the use of the technology has been obtained by a license or any other agreement with a patent owner, are there any terms in the agreement that would terminate or otherwise impose a limit on the right as a result of entering into this transaction? For example, is the right under the agreement fully transferable; are there preliminary conditions to be met before transfer; or are any rights altered upon the transfer according to the terms of the agreement? Are there any limitations on the license such as a field-of-use limitation, a geographical limitation, or any clause calling for premature termination of the license upon the occurrence of particular events? Are there any dominating patents held by the patent owner or others, i.e., is the license sufficient to provide a full right to use, or does the practice of the licensed technology require the use of materials, components, methods, or processes that are covered by other patents not included in the license?

Ability to Exclude Others

1. Are the products or technology of interest in the transaction covered by patents to which the target has exclusive rights? If

the transaction extends to sales or operations in countries outside the United States, does the patent coverage include patent coverage in these countries as well?

2. Are the patents fully owned by the target? To answer this question, the investigator will explore the following:

   (a.) Have all patents been assigned to the target by the inventors?

   (b.) For technology not yet patented, are all the inventors employees of the target, and have all employees executed employment agreements that obligate employees to assign to the target the patent rights to inventions that the employees invent while employed? Do the agreements require the employees who have left the target's employ to continue to assist the target in obtaining patents on inventions that they conceived during their employment?

   (c.) Are any of the patents the result of joint inventions between employees of the target and outside individuals? Have those individuals assigned their rights to the target? Are there any inventorship disputes with outside contractors or other outside parties?

3. Are all patents currently in force and free of any challenges or doubts to their validity? Have all maintenance fees been paid and is there an adequate system for tracking the due dates of future maintenance fees? Have there been any post issuance matters such as oppositions, reissues, and reexaminations? Has anyone expressed the belief that the patents are invalid or more limited in scope than they appear to be?

4. When do the patents expire?

5. Are the claims of the patents broad enough to provide the target with an effective market advantage rather than simply covering the target's own products?

6. Has all information in the possession of the target that is relevant to the validity of a patent been supplied to the United States Patent and Trademark Office (USPTO)?

7. If patent rights have been obtained from a patentee who is not an employee of the target, were those rights obtained by assignment or license? If by license, is the license exclusive or nonexclusive? Does the license contain any special provisions relating to the assertion of the patent over infringers?

8. Has any other party applied for a patent on an invention for which the target has also applied, or on inventions that are overlapping or highly similar to those of the target? Have there been any interferences or notifications of the possibility of an interference?

9. Has any infringement by outside parties been discovered or suspected?

Continual attention to all of these questions during normal operations is often impractical for a company with more than a few patents, but certain organizational practices can help assure that answers to these questions can be readily obtained when due diligence is initiated. Prominent among these is a patent-organizing system including a patent status list, maintained and periodically updated by a responsible staff person, itemizing all patents and patent applications that the company has applied for, both United States and abroad, and the current status of each. The list should correlate the patents with the company's products or services so that the coverage for any given product or service can be readily identified.

In addition to the list, a separate file should be maintained for each patent, containing copies of all documents received from or sent to the USPTO, assignments of the patent to company, communications with outside counsel regarding the patent, and communications with competitors, licensees, and other outside parties regarding the patent. All investigations, analyses, and opinions relating to nonpatented subject matter should also be stored in an indexed fashion. The same should be true for all employment agreements and copies of company policies relating to intellectual property, as well as signed copies of all licenses, assignments, options, or other agreements with competitors and business partners.

INTELLECTUAL PROPERTY BEYOND PATENTS

While patent rights typically constitute the largest portion of intellectual property due diligence, other forms of intellectual property can be investigated as well.

Confidentiality and trade secret rights typically appear in confidential disclosure agreements, including those that visitors to the company are required to sign upon entry, as well as those required of company employees. Confidential disclosure agreements are also executed with potential business partners to protect the parties during the investigation stages that precede the parties' entry into transactions such as licenses, joint ventures, or other strategic alliances. All such documents should be maintained in an organized manner that will allow them to be found when needed. Lists of trademarks, service marks, trade names, and domain names should be maintained, together with files containing the appropriate documentation for each. Documentation showing that the target has been consistently enforcing its marks should also be maintained since it will be useful in the event that it becomes necessary to defend the marks. Trademark availability searches and correspondence and other documentation relating to trademark disputes or confrontations should likewise be maintained, as should copyright registrations and correspondence relating to any copyright disputes.

Chapter 2

What Is Patentable? Mining the Technology Platform

For most corporations, the patent portfolio is more than a book of wares or a list of assets; it is the foundation of the corporation's identity, the corporation's ability to compete in the marketplace, and the corporation's ability to generate revenue. The greater the number and diversity of a corporation's patents, the stronger the foundation. The foundation can be built and strengthened by encouraging and even exhorting employees to invent, but it can be built and strengthened more effectively by simply understanding the broad range of subject matter that qualifies for patent protection and recognizing and identifying patentable inventions as they arise. The creativity, ingenuity, and resourcefulness that are readily applied in technical matters can be applied to patenting as well, and often the only limits to the scope of a patent portfolio are preconceived notions of what can or cannot be patented. This chapter demonstrates that there are essentially no limits to the types of invention that can be patented.

PATENTABLE SUBJECT MATTER

The official source and statement of the patent right and of what can be patented is the patent statute, Title 35 of the United States Code, Section 101. The breadth of possibilities for patent coverage is not particularly evident from the statute, however, which reads as follows:

§101. Inventions Patentable
Whoever invents or discovers any new and useful process, machine, manufacture, or composition of matter, or any new and useful improvement

thereof, may obtain a patent therefor, subject to the conditions and requirements of this title.

While the "conditions and requirements" are addressed elsewhere in this book, the four categories—process, machine, manufacture, and composition of matter—are not as limiting as they might appear, since patent law, like law in general, has the ability to adapt itself to changing times. The scope of patentable subject matter has thus been reinterpreted repeatedly to incorporate emerging technologies, economic realities, and changing scenarios in commerce and industry. The reinterpretation occurs through the courts and the changing policies of the United States Patent and Trademark Office (USPTO) itself. In fact, so many different varieties of inventions have been deemed to qualify for patents over the years that the four categories listed in the statute now serve more as an introduction to the essentially limitless range of patentable subject matter than as a set of boundaries.

Here are some examples of the types of inventions that are currently recognized by the USPTO and the patent courts as qualifying for patents under the four categories listed in the statute:

"Process"—this term encompasses "method" (with patent law drawing no distinction between the two)

- manufacturing processes defined by a specified combination or sequence of steps, or by a particular operation on a particular material or component
- manufacturing processes defined by the conditions of manufacture or treatment—for example, exposure to a specified environment such as temperature, pressure, oxidizing or nonoxidizing atmosphere, acidic or alkaline conditions, vapor-phase versus liquid phase, supercritical conditions, plasma conditions, electric potential, magnetic field, heating or cooling rate, and time factors such as exposure time, residence time, or aging time or conditions
- manufacturing processes defined by the use of specified raw materials or raw materials in a specified condition such as particle size, purity, or surface qualities
- manufacturing processes defined by the equipment used
- chemical processes such as synthesis reactions or reaction sequences, raw material treatment processes, and product recovery and purification processes

- electronic processes such as signal generation, signal transmission, signal processing, switching, and methods of feedback and control

- methods of treating living organisms (including therapeutic, preventive, or other medical uses; enhancement methods such as memory or performance enhancing or methods affecting physiological responses to drug administration or other externally imposed conditions; and cosmetic methods and procedures)

- methods of treating materials (including surface treatments; toughening treatments; treatments to control or change crystal structure or molecular arrangement; bonding, welding, or fusing methods; etching methods; deposition methods; masking methods; printing methods; and cleaning and sterilization methods)

- methods of treating soil, water, or air, or the environment in general, for purposes of decontamination, remediation, purification, waste treatment, disposal, or recycling, or for purposes of enhancing a property such as fertility, potability, or ecosystem support

- methods of use (including the use of particular equipment or materials on particular substrates, raw materials, or workpieces; and uses of chemicals or biological species for clinical, therapeutic, diagnostic, agricultural, industrial, or consumer use, including drugs, microbes, catalysts, and additives or formulating agents in general)

- testing methods for materials and equipment, such as methods for quality control, methods for assessing performance under specified conditions, calibration methods, and standardization methods

- soil, water, or air quality testing, including methods to detect bacteria levels, carcinogens, chemical oxygen demand, biological oxygen demand, toxicity factors in general, particulate level, dissolved solids, and plant emissions

- analytical methods, including clinical laboratory procedures for diagnosis, treatment monitoring, and general health care, and methods for use by analytical laboratories for determination or verification of chemical structure, or for yield or purity determinations

- screening methods, such as high-volume or high-throughput screening of pharmaceutical candidates or agents for affinity binding or for their impact on biochemical and physiological pathways
- business methods, including accounting methods, inventory methods, billing methods, forecasting methods, marketing methods, selling methods, electronic commerce methods, methods for information control and management, combinations of interacting business components or units, data processing in general, and software

"Machine" and "manufacture"

- machines or complete pieces of equipment or components of machines and equipment, whether powered or not powered and with or without moving parts, to be used in consumer products, recreational products, products for industrial use, or products used in the manufacture of consumer products or products for industrial use
- materials of construction such as plastics, alloys, ceramics, adhesives, agglomerates, laminates, membranes, castings, reinforced materials, and structural components in general
- electronic devices and microelectromechanical systems (MEMS), including circuitry, chip architecture, circuit boards, and electronic packages
- medical devices, including implants, prostheses, catheters, stents, surgical tools, monitoring devices, and corrective devices

"Composition of matter"

- chemical compositions, including chemical species, complexes, constructs, mixtures, laminates, coatings, solutions, suspensions, emulsions, and combinations in general, such as pharmaceutical and cosmetic formulations, data storage and recording media, and electronic transmission media and magnetic recording or storage media, or digital recording or storage media
- biological systems and species, including macromolecules, nucleic acids, gene sequences, proteins and protein analogs, living cells, and culture media

- chemical compositions prepared by specified processes, particularly those that are difficult to characterize other than by the manner in which they were prepared

This is by no means a limiting list, but it should be clear from the breadth of these examples that one would have much more difficulty naming a subject-matter type that does not qualify for patent protection than taking a particular invention and classifying it within one of the categories in the list. One is compelled to conclude that attempting to fit a particular invention into one of the four classes set forth in the statute is neither necessary nor advisable. Instead, one needs only to identify whether an innovation provides a benefit of any kind: presenting new possibilities; providing an improvement over an existing product, material, or way of doing things; or even merely offering an alternative to something that already exists. Such an innovation should then be considered a possibly patentable invention.

EXPANDING COVERAGE WITH MULTIPLE APPROACHES

Full market exclusivity for a line of products or services, a technology platform, or proprietary matter in general can be secured by patents that cover each of the features, aspects, or embodiments of the proprietary matter that competitors might otherwise appropriate. A single patent can cover two or more distinct products or services if the products or services can be generically expressed as separate embodiments of a unifying concept. The reverse is true as well, however: a single product or service can be covered by two or more patents. With imagination, a recognition of the possibilities, and an appreciation of the values of different types of inventions that qualify for patents, a single product can lead to a broad and powerful patent base.

A core discovery of a particular quality of a material or a functional part, for example, can lead to one patent on components that put the discovery to functional use, another patent on larger units that incorporate the components and use them for performing larger tasks, a third patent on methods of using the units to perform the tasks, and a fourth patent on methods of using the component in contexts or scenarios beyond those of the larger units. The discovery of a previously unrecognized quality in a known material—whether the material is a molecular substance; a chemical, metallurgical, or biochemical composition, naturally occurring or otherwise; or a substance that has been treated in a particular way—may make the material useful in numerous ways beyond its previously known use. This can lead to separate patents on each of the uses as well as patents on compositions that contain the substance and are specially formulated for each use.

An illustration of a product covered by a multitude of patents and a multitude of different types of claims is a single diagnostic device that determines whether a woman complaining of certain gynecological symptoms is suffering from bacterial vaginosis or from some condition other than bacterial vaginosis. The device is a laminated plastic card the size of a credit card. The card is constructed such that when a specimen of vaginal fluid is applied to the surface of the card, certain indicia will appear on the card only when bacterial vaginosis is present. The card thus enables a woman or her physician to avoid administering the wrong medications for her symptoms and it lets the woman or physician know when further testing is needed to determine the actual cause of the symptoms.

The card tests two characteristics of the specimen—the acidity of the specimen and the presence in the specimen of salts of a particular type of amine—and utilizes two fundamental discoveries relating to the means of detecting these characteristics.

One of the discoveries is that if a particular type of pH (acidity) indicator is dispersed within a particular type of polymer, the indicator becomes highly sensitive in the pH range where the threshold acidity indicative of bacterial vaginosis resides. This led to Patent No. 5,897,834, which contains two sets of claims. One set (claims 1–12) is directed to the indicator/polymer combination itself, while the other (claims 13–33) is directed to a laminated plastic construction that includes the indicator/polymer combination in one layer and an indicator without the particular polymer in another layer. With these two layers, two distinct indicia can result: one formed by color changes in both of the layers and the other by a color change in the second layer only, depending on the specimen. A specimen with enough acidity to indicate bacterial vaginosis thus produces changes in both layers in the form of a plus sign while a specimen with lesser acidity produces a change only in the second layer, forming a minus sign by leaving out one of the two bars of the plus sign. In addition to increasing the sensitivity of the indicator in the critical range, the polymer offers the extra benefit of being able to hold the pH indicator in place even when the layers are wetted with a liquid specimen. This led to Patent No. 6,113,856, in which the invention is recited as a method of immobilizing the indicator in a solid layer so that the indicator will not bleed, specifying use of the special polymer as the solid layer.

Another discovery was embodied in the portion of the device that detects salts of a particular type of amine. The amine salts of interest are salts of volatile amines rather than salts of amines that are not volatile. To differentiate between the two, the inventors have devised a way to liberate the amines from the salts and to place an amine indicator inside a solid material that is penetrable by gas but not liquid. Thus, when the specimen is applied to the card, an observable change in the indicator means that salts of volatile amines are present in the specimen since only the volatile amines could reach the indicator. This led to Patent No. 6,099,801 which claims a test device that incorporates the amine-liberating feature and the embedded indicator.

Still further patents covering the same test card address the pH-related features and the amine-related features as a combination. Patent No. 5,660,790 claims a test device that incorporates the features of both tests, and Patent No. 5,910,447 claims a method for diagnosing bacterial vaginosis by using a test device that incorporates the features. The test card is therefore covered by five patents and six sets of claims, all claiming different aspects of a single test device, which is a laminated plastic card the size of a credit card. The advantage of having all these patents and different types of claims is that they offer a broad scope of patent protection, extending beyond the test device itself and the disease to which the test device is directed, and they also offer a variety of options from both offensive and defensive strategies. Thus, if a competitor later develops an alternative for one of the two tests that falls outside the patent coverage for that test, a patent on the remaining test will be still be assertible against the competitor. Likewise, if one of the two discoveries is later found to have already been published elsewhere in a manner rendering the claims to that discovery unenforceable, the claims to the remaining discovery will still be effective. Thus, the different patents and claims provide the patent holder with different ways to approach infringers, different infringers that the patents can be asserted over, different licensing strategies, different royalty bases, and different types of backup support in the event that any one set of claims is challenged or found to be unenforceable.

HOW MUCH PATENT COVERAGE IS ENOUGH?

Even in situations where a single patent is sufficient to exclude competition, the question remains: What value can there be to having multiple patents covering the same product if the competition is fully excluded by a single patent? Likewise, the amount of a product-based royalty in a license agreement is generally not dependent on the number of patents that the product falls under; so here again, what value is there to multiple patents?

One reason for multiple patent coverage is that a patent is enforceable for only a limited period of time, with an expiration date determined while the patent application is pending. Although a number of factors can influence the expiration date, the term of a patent is not extendable or renewable beyond that date. When a particular product or process is covered by a number of patents issued on successive dates, however, each patent may have an independent expiration date, effectively passing coverage from one patent to the next as each earlier-issued patent expires. This frequently occurs in products or services whose development has occurred in stages. In the typical stage-wise scenario, a fundamental or breakthrough invention is followed by successive discoveries, expansions, or improvements, each relating to one or more aspects of the original invention and either making the invention more effective for particular uses or results, or making it easier or less expensive to manufacture, perform, or implement, or offering any benefit that adds to its value. Typically, each discovery or improvement is incorporated into products or processes that utilize the original invention soon after the discovery or improvement arises, and each constitutes a patentable advance relative to the product or process as it existed prior to the discovery or improvement. New patent filings at each stage produce a succession of patents, each one valid and enforceable and yet independent of its predecessors, and the term of each patent will extend beyond that of its immediate predecessor.

Another reason for multiple patent coverage is flexibility in dealing with unforeseen obstacles and challenges. Challenges to a patent or patent application can arise at any time and from any source, and certain challenges can be fatal. Pending patent applications can be amended to meet some of these challenges, while an issued patent has fewer options. A patent can be particularly vulnerable when challenged by an aggressive competitor that has more resources than the USPTO and a particular interest in having the patent declared invalid. Proving that a single patent is invalid can be a much simpler task than doing so for a multitude of patents, however, particularly when the various patents claim the invention in different ways. Even if the validity of a patent is unchallenged or challenged unsuccessfully, efforts to enforce a patent can be thwarted by disputes over the scope of the patent and by attempts to design or engineer around a patent. Avoiding or designing around a multitude of patents is generally much more difficult than avoiding or designing around a single patent.

MARKET PERSPECTIVES

A useful way to develop broad patent coverage from an invention is to claim the invention with a view toward commercial activities and industries external to those of the inventor and the inventor's employer. This broader perspective can be gained by focusing on questions such as:

1. What competitive activities do I wish to control or eliminate by my patent coverage?
2. What activities could others in the industry or in related industries engage in that might erode market power that the invention creates or lessen the value added by the invention?
3. What industries other than my own might benefit from the invention?
4. What are the greatest possibilities for licensing or royalty fees from the invention?

Broad coverage is obtained by looking beyond what the inventor has actually constructed or tests that the inventor has actually performed and data that the inventor has actually generated. If the invention is a product, market power is certainly gained by excluding competitors from marketing the same product or products embodying the same inventive concept. More effective protection can often be gained however by excluding those who supply materials or kits from which the product is made or assembled, or those who supply other products or units made from the product in question. The product may be useful in certain processing or manufacturing steps in unrelated industries, or it may be more valuable when transformed into a more finished product. If the invention resides in a process, whether it is a screening process, a treatment process, or a conversion, its greatest market impact may be among those who utilize the product resulting from the screening, treatment, or conversion.

Awareness of the various commercial activities competitors might engage in should be coupled with an awareness of which competitors and industries have the largest financial resources and how the invention might be cast to encompass their activities and thereby reap the greatest financial reward from the invention. Geographical and boundary-crossing considerations will also affect the patenting strategy. For example, patent enforcement may be difficult in countries where the invention is directly copied. It may be possible to overcome this obstacle by claiming the invention in ways that will encompass activities in other countries where the original infringer is doing business. This can arise when a patented assembly is made from parts that are manufactured in one country and assembled in another where the patent is less likely to be enforced. It can also arise when a patented process is performed in a remote jurisdiction and only the product is imported into the more accessible jurisdiction.

Strategic business considerations can therefore enter into the identification of inventions and the manner in which inventions are claimed. These considerations, coupled with a recognition of and sensitivity toward the essentially limitless boundaries of patentable subject matter and a creative collaboration between the inventor and the patent attorney, can help build a solid patent foundation.

Chapter 3

The Power to Exclude: Claim Scope and Strategy

While a patent is in force, it is a legal instrument, and its value and effect as a legal instrument reside in its claims. Each claim defines what the patent holder, with the support of the judiciary, can exclude others from doing, and each can serve as the basis for royalties in licensing arrangements under the patent. As a set, the claims embody the strategies available to the patent holder for enforcing and defending the patent, and yet they are also responsible for the risk of a loss of rights under the patent.

THE CLAIMS VERSUS THE SPECIFICATION

Despite their role in demarcating the patent holder's rights against others, the claims are presented in a fairly unobtrusive manner, appearing at the end of the patent, after the abstract, drawings, and text, with no visual emphasis or even much if any spatial separation from the remaining text, nor even a subheading to show the reader where they begin. Subheadings typically appear throughout the remainder of the patent, the most typical being "BACKGROUND OF THE INVENTION," "SUMMARY OF THE INVENTION," "BRIEF DE-SCRIPTION OF THE DRAWINGS," and "DESCRIPTION OF THE PREFERRED EMBODIMENTS," each in all capital letters, centered, and set apart from the text above and below with white space. By contrast, the first claim is typically preceded only by the words

"What is claimed is:" without capitalization, a change in font, or extra space above or below.

In some patents, this lack of emphasis is aggravated by misleading impressions from more prominent portions of the patent. The "SUMMARY OF THE INVENTION," for example, typically begins in the first or second column of the first page of the patent. In some patents the summary is stated in broad terms, implying that the patent coverage extends over a range of activity that is broader than what the claims actually cover. Other summaries list features that are not requirements in the broadest claims, thereby suggesting that the coverage is narrower than it actually is. Illustrations of both are found in Patent No. 6,312,605, which is directed to a process and apparatus for treating contaminated soil formations or groundwater by injecting an oxidizing gas (the prime example being ozone) into the site of contamination. Two paragraphs from the SUMMARY OF THE INVENTION are quoted below.

> [Opening paragraph:] The present invention relates to injection of oxidizing gas in the form of microfine bubbles into aquifer regions by means of a sparging system which includes one or more injection wells to encourage in-situ remediation of sub-surface leachate plumes by means of a gas-gas-water reaction. The present invention is directed to sparging systems and methods of in-situ groundwater remediation in combination with co-reactant substrate materials acting as a catalyst to encourage biodegradation of leachate plumes for removal of dissolved chlorinated hydrocarbons and dissolved hydrocarbon petroleum products. Remediation of saturated soils may also be obtained by employment of the present invention. In particular the present invention employs sparging apparatus including microporous bubble generators for generating micron-sized duo-gas bubbles into aquifer regions by means of one or more vertically arranged injection wells having a bubble chamber for regulating the size of bubbles. The sparging system of the present invention encourages biodegradation of leachate plumes which contain biodegradable organics or Criegee decomposition of leachate plumes containing dissolved chlorinated hydrocarbons.
>
> [Sixth paragraph:] In the present invention, the concept of the microfine sparge system manipulation is predicated upon a thorough knowledge of the features of the groundwater or saturated zones on a site selected for remediation. Balancing the volume of air to the microfine system sparge loci enables control of sparging efficiency and balancing of any downgradient movement of a contaminated plume while remediation is accomplished. Critical to microfine sparge system design and accomplishment of any of the above points is to initially perform a "sparge point test" for the purpose of evaluating the characteristics of the site for matching purposes.

Claim 1 of this patent reads as follows (emphasis added):

> 1. A process for removing contaminants, including dissolved chlorinated hydrocarbons and dissolved hydrocarbon products, said process comprising:
>
> evaluating a site to identify contaminants present on the site;
>
> installing an infection [*sic*, injection] well system and sparge system including a sparge apparatus at each injection well of said well system;
>
> selecting an appropriate bubble size range for gaseous exchange with the contaminants, by matching the bubble size range with characteristics of the sparge apparatus and microporous material used with the sparge apparatus in accordance with results obtained from evaluating the site;
>
> controlling a supply of gas, said gas including an oxidizing gas, while injecting the gas into the site, and *alternating water injection with bubble production* to provide an even dispersion of bubbles, to promote pulling of the contaminants into the bubbles and to decompose the contaminants in a reaction with the gas in the bubbles in the presence of water; and
>
> enhancing decomposition of the contaminants by carrying out the reaction *in the presence of a reaction promoter.*

As the italicized sections indicate, infringement of this claim requires, among the other steps that the claim recites, "alternating water injection with bubble production" and "carrying out the reaction in the presence of a reaction promoter." Neither of these is mentioned in paragraphs quoted above from the "SUMMARY," or in any other paragraphs of the "SUMMARY." The SUMMARY thus fails to inform the reader that infringement of Claim 1 can be *avoided* either by injecting water and producing bubbles *simultaneously* rather than alternately, or by not including a reaction promoter, or both.

Since Claim 1 is only one of four independent claims of the patent, the knowledgeable reader will ask whether the inconsistencies between Claim 1 and the SUMMARY are compensated for in the other three independent claims, Claims 12, 19 and 27. A review of Claims 12, 19 and 27 reveals that the "alternating" limitation is present in these claims as well, while the "reaction promoter" limitation is present in Claims 12 and 27 but not in Claim 19. Thus, any of the four independent claims can be avoided by injecting water producing bubbles simultaneously. As will be explained below, this means that *none* of the claims in the patent will be infringed unless these steps are performed alternately rather than simultaneously.

Claims 19 and 27, however, both contain an *additional* limitation that is not stated in the SUMMARY, and yet are *missing* still further limitations that *are* stated in the SUMMARY. Claim 19 is illustrative (emphasis added):

> 19. A process for removing contaminants, including dissolved chlorinated hydrocarbons and dissolved hydrocarbon products, said process comprising:
> injecting gas including an oxidizing gas, into the site; and
> alternating water injection with bubble production to provide an even dispersion of bubbles, *with the bubbles having a bubble diameter in a range of about 5 to 200 microns* to promote pulling of contaminants into the bubbles and to decompose the contaminants in a reaction with the gas in the bubbles in the presence of water.

The additional limitation is the limitation of the bubble diameter to a range of 5 to 200 microns, a range not mentioned anywhere in the SUMMARY. The missing limitations are the evaluation step and the matching of the bubble-size range with the characteristics of the sparge apparatus and microporous materials, steps that the SUMMARY identifies as "critical" (see the sixth paragraph of the SUMMARY, quoted above). Claim 19 is thus *narrower* than the SUMMARY suggests in terms of the bubble-size range, and *broader* than the SUMMARY suggests in terms of the evaluation and matching steps, i.e., the SUMMARY fails to inform the reader that omitting the "critical" evaluation and matching steps will *not* result in avoiding infringement of the patent. In several respects, therefore, the claim coverage as a whole is inconsistent with the SUMMARY.

These inconsistencies do not make the patent invalid, nor do they necessarily reflect an effort on the part of the patent drafter to deceive the reader, since claims are frequently amended or canceled, and new claims added, while the patent application is pending. The inconsistencies do however indicate the complexities of claim evaluation, a topic addressed in some detail below.

THE FUNCTION OF A CLAIM

In its everyday use, the word "claim" is typically associated with a statement, whether supported by fact or not, declaring the virtues, uniqueness, advantages, or benefits of something. In the context of a patent, however, the word serves a different and more specific purpose: a patent claim delineates in precise terms the scope of what the patent owner can exclude others from doing. This allows

Patent-Type Claims	Nonpatent-Type Claims
1. Apparatus for injecting a reactive gas into a soil formation, comprising an outer length of hollow tubing having a side wall with openings less than 200 microns in diameter; and an inner length of hollow tubing disposed within said outer length, said inner length having a side wall with openings less than 200 microns in diameter.	1. Apparatus for injecting a reactive gas into a soil formation, which can remove contaminants from said formation without the need for drawing a vacuum on said formation.
2. The apparatus of claim 1 further comprising a common end cap to seal the downstream ends of both lengths of hollow tubing and a common inlet cap with separate openings leading to the interior of said inner length of tubing and the annular space between said inner and outer lengths of tubing.	2. The apparatus of claim 1 which can remove contaminants from said formation to the same degree as vacuum methods but in less than half the time.
3. The apparatus of claim 1 further comprising porous packing material disposed in the annular space between said inner and outer lengths of tubing.	3. The apparatus of claim 1 which can be operated without releasing contaminants from the soil formation into the air.
4. The apparatus of claim 1 wherein said inner and outer lengths of tubing are coaxial circular cylinders.	4. The apparatus of claim 1 which is the first such apparatus to produce intimate mixing of said reactive gas with said contaminants.

others operating in the field to determine from reading the claim what activities they can engage in without being subject to liability to the patent holder for infringement. A comparison of the two sets of "claims" (all fictitious) shown above illustrates the distinction.

Each of the "patent-type claims" shown above sets forth the features that a gas-injecting apparatus must contain if it is to infringe that claim, letting the potential infringer know which features to look for in the infringer's own apparatus. If the apparatus contains all of the features in one claim, that claim will be infringed, whereas if one or more of the features is missing, that claim will not be infringed. None of the "nonpatent-type claims" listed above provide the potential infringer with this type of information. If Claim 1 of the latter were to actually appear in a patent, for example, the claim would presume to cover all soil remediation equipment that does not involve vacuum extraction. Claim 2 would likewise presume to cover all soil remediation equipment that is twice as fast as vacuum extraction for every type of soil formation, and so on for Claims 3 and 4. These excessively broad scopes would most likely not have been the intention of the inventor, nor would they be supportable by the descriptions in the patent of actual units that the inventor had constructed.

THE SCOPE OF A CLAIM

With the high cost of obtaining patent protection and the potentially high value of a patent as a competitive tool in the business environment, the patent holder should have a thorough understanding of the scope of coverage afforded by its patents. The purpose of a claim is to define the full range of activities that the patent holder can prevent others from performing without the patent holder's permission, rather than to describe what the inventor has actually performed or constructed. The claims are indeed based on the inventor's actual work or an outgrowth of this work, but when properly drafted, the claims will extend beyond the inventor's work to encompass the full reach of reasonable implications that the inventor's work suggests. Claim drafting therefore typically involves a significant amount of speculation in selecting the appropriate scope. The patent attorney will urge the inventor to think in extended terms and to use generic rather than specific expressions for as many aspects of the invention as the invention will support from a technological standpoint. This expansive thinking will be balanced by the attorney's knowledge of how much expansion will be legally supportable from the standpoint of patent law.

The term "limitations," as suggested above, is the legal term for the language in a claim that defines the boundaries establishing the dividing lines between infringing and noninfringing activity. Most limitations are negative in nature: a claim is narrower in scope for their presence, and the more limitations the narrower the scope. When a claim recites a feature without accompanying limitations or avoids reciting the feature entirely, that feature will play no role in the scope of activity that will infringe that claim. For example, when height is mentioned in the claim but no height limitation is expressed, or when height is not mentioned at all, infringing activity is not limited to any particular height (any height will infringe). Likewise, where there is no exposure time limitation, any exposure time will infringe, and where there is no quantity limitation, any quantity will infringe. When a claim fails to recite a component, infringement does not depend on whether or not the component is present; and when a process step is not recited, infringement will not depend on whether or not the step is performed. These results can all be modified by inserting explicit language in the claim, but in general, this means that the fewer the limitations, which often means the shorter the claim, the broader the scope.

To illustrate, consider the following (fictitious) claim:

A process for upgrading petroleum distillation bottoms, comprising:

A.) combining said distillation bottoms with an aqueous liquid to form a dispersion;

B.) treating said dispersion by irradiation with ultrasound sufficient to convert components of said distillation bottoms to lower-boiling species; and

C.) recovering the organic phase from said dispersion thus treated.

Any process applied to petroleum distillation bottoms that involves the performance of steps (A), (B), and (C) will fall within the scope of this claim. Note that the proportion of distillation bottoms to aqueous fluid is not stated, and hence there are no limits on the relative amounts of each. The term "aqueous liquid" is recognized among chemists to mean either water itself or a solution formed by dissolving nonwater chemical species in water, and both water and any such solution are encompassed by the claim. Neither the intensity nor duration of the ultrasound is recited, and hence any intensity and duration that will convert at least some of the components to lower-boiling species will be encompassed by the claim. There are no recitations of preheating the distillation bottoms prior to combining them with the aqueous liquid or to agitating the combined liquids to form the dispersion. As a result, processes that include these steps as well as those that avoid them will all be encompassed by the claim. Similar results apply to such features as the presence or absence of additives to stabilize the dispersion, the number of distillation bottom components that are converted to lower-boiling species, the degree to which the boiling points are lowered, whether the process is performed in a batchwise manner or a continuous manner, and all of the various other parameters that systems of this type entail.

Compare the above claim with the following:

A process for upgrading petroleum distillation bottoms, comprising:

A.) heating said distillation bottoms to a temperature exceeding 150°C;

B.) combining said distillation bottoms thus heated with an aqueous liquid and a nonionic surfactant to form an dispersion;

C.) contacting said dispersion with a transition metal catalyst;

D.) treating said dispersion, while in contact with said catalyst, with ultrasound sufficient to convert components of said distillation bottoms to lower-boiling species;

E.) separating the dispersion thus treated into aqueous and organic phases; and

F.) recycling the aqueous phase from said dispersion to step (b).

This seven-step claim contains all the limitations of the preceding three-step claim plus additional limitations (in the form of additional steps). With these additional limitations, the seven-step claim, despite its greater length, is narrower in scope than the three-step claim.

MULTIPLE CLAIMS AND CLAIMING STRATEGIES

A patent must contain at least one claim to be legally complete, and a single claim will meet the statutory requirement that "the specification shall conclude with one or more claims particularly pointing out and distinctly claiming the subject matter that the applicant claims as his invention." (35 U.S.C. § 112, second paragraph.) Most patents however contain a multitude of claims. Regardless of the number, claims are individually operative: if the patent holder can show that an unauthorized activity or product falls within the scope of any single claim, infringement is established. Infringement liability is not a matter of degree—liability is no greater when more claims are infringed. An activity or product is either infringing or not infringing.

Patent law requires that no two claims in a single patent be identical in scope. The difference however may be very slight or not readily apparent. Different claims can overlap, and broad overlaps are not only common but also useful to the patent holder. The reasons for including a number of claims rather than a single claim, and for including broad overlaps among the claims, are to provide the patent holder with (1) options and flexibility when arguing the patentability of the claims before an examiner or asserting the patent over an infringer, and (2) resiliency when one or more claims are declared invalid or unenforceable, either by an examiner or a court of law. An important feature of claims is that when one or more, but less than all, claims of a patent are deemed invalid, the invalidity does not apply to the remaining claims unless the same reason for invalidity applies to them as well. A patent is thus strengthened and less vulnerable to attack when the patent holder has a large number of claims to choose from in a legal action against an infringer.

With a set of different claims, the patent holder can build a variety of risk levels into the patent. Claims of broad scope carry a relatively high risk since their breadth tends to make these claims more vulnerable to challenge. The challenge may arise from a late discovery of an activity or product that falls within the scope of the claim and, although unknown to the inventor, was already in the public domain at the time the invention was made, thereby depriving the claim of novelty. Even inventors who make efforts to stay abreast of commercial and developmental activity in their fields are susceptible to these late discoveries since no individual can monitor everything. Thus, a commercial-scale plant operation that includes units or process steps that were not on display for public viewing, a publication in an obscure journal, a doctoral thesis deposited in a university library and not otherwise circulated, or a host of other such obscure activities can be found by an aggressive challenger who has a substantial interest in having the patent declared invalid and the resources to search on a wide scale. The challenge can also arise from a late discovery that the invention is not operative, or its benefits not realized, over the full scope of the claim, suggesting that the conceptual extension of the inventor's work as expressed in the claim was too optimistic or not sufficiently justified by the limited data that the inventor actually obtained.

Each of these vulnerabilities declines with claims of lesser scope while the range of infringing activities declines as well. The result is a trade-off between risk and range.

Different claims also provide the patent holder with different strategies for generating revenue. Some strategies are fully served by a claim of relatively narrow range. The patent may be licensed, for example, for a specific use which the licensee cannot modify or can do so only under economically unfavorable conditions. Similarly, the aim of the patent holder may simply be to obtain a market position in a narrowly defined market. A narrow claim will serve both these purposes while offering low vulnerability to challenge. Other strategies are best served by broad claims. The patent holder may for example seek a proprietary position in an emerging technology, or may believe that the invention has the ability to influence or add value to areas and applications that have so far received only a limited exploration. While a broad range of applications offers considerable potential for income generation, the inventor or the inventor's employer may lack the funding, labor, or time to fully develop the invention and investigate all of its possibilities before applying for a patent. The need for breadth can be particularly acute when the inventor's work involves a fundamental discovery that can readily be extended by other investigators once they see the inventor's results. By its nature, this type of invention deserves a broad scope, and a claim that does not extend much beyond the inventor's own work will have limited value.

Claim breadth is also a concern among patent applicants who are compelled to obtain early filing dates for their patent applications. Measured against the rapid pace of innovation in today's technologies, the term of enforceability of a patent seems long, extending to a date twenty years from the date that the patent was first applied for. In rapidly evolving technologies, therefore, the patent may have its greatest value in the earlier years of its term, and this can suggest that the expiration date is of less concern than the need to explore the full scope of the discovery and all of its implications before preparing the patent application. An early filing date may be necessary, however, to avoid a loss of patent rights. This can occur, for example, when the laboratory test results have already been submitted for publication, when licensing revenue from the invention is needed at an early date to fund further research, or when the invention must be disclosed to a funding agency in a nonconfidential manner. In these cases, vulnerability to challenge is influenced not only by the breadth of a claim but also by the filing date of the application. The inventor's comfort level may also be a factor in accommodating the seemingly competing interests of breadth versus filing date. Inventors frequently have concerns about whether their inventions are truly operable over a broad range without further testing, or they may feel that their professional reputation is at stake if they claim a breadth that greatly exceeds their actual work.

A patent therefore needs to provide its owner with flexibility and strategic advantages in licensing and in asserting the patent over infringers, and yet to contain protection from any of the various challenges that patents can encounter. To accommodate these interests, the well-prepared patent typically includes a variety of different claims, ranging from broad to narrow, with numerous claims of intermediate breadth in between. The scope array is achieved by adding a variety of increasingly conservative limitations on the features and parameters of the invention or on the environment in which the invention is practiced.

INDEPENDENT AND DEPENDENT CLAIMS

To make the task of reading and analyzing a large number of claims less cumbersome for both the patent examiner and the potential infringer, claims are typically written as a combination of independent and dependent claims. An independent claim is self-contained with no cross-reference to any other claim, while a dependent claim contains an explicit cross-reference to another (lower-numbered) claim, generally within the first few words of the claim. The result may appear as follows:

...

2. The apparatus of claim 1...

...

8. A process in accordance with claim 6...

...

12. A product prepared by the process of claim 10...

The effect of this cross-referencing is that all of the limitations of the referenced claim (Claims 1, 6, and 10 in these examples) are incorporated into the referencing claim (Claims 2, 8, and 12). The referenced claim can be either an independent claim or another dependent claim, provided that any successive dependencies (chain-type cross-referencing) terminate at an independent claim. When the dependencies lead through one or more dependent ("intervening") claims before reaching the ultimate independent ("base") claim, all of the limitations recited in all of the claims in the series are incorporated into the first claim in the dependency chain, i.e., the claim furthest removed along the chain from the base claim.

Of the four "Patent-Type Claims" listed above ("Apparatus for injecting a reactive gas into a soil formation..."), Claim 1 is independent and Claims 2, 3, and 4 are dependent. Claim 1 covers any reactive gas injection apparatus that includes inner and outer lengths of hollow tubing each having side walls with openings less than 200 microns in diameter, regardless of any other structural components or features included in (or missing from) the apparatus. Claim 2 incorporates all of these limitations and adds the limitation of a common end cap and a common inlet cap (as opposed to, for example, individual end caps for each of the two lengths of tubing, individual inlet caps, or both). To infringe Claim 2, therefore, the apparatus must contain not only the inner and outer lengths of tubing with the appropriately sized openings, but also the common end cap and common inlet cap. Claim 3 likewise incorporates all of the limitations of Claim 1 (the inner and outer tubing lengths and the side-wall openings of specified maximum diameter) and adds the limitation of the porous packing material. Claim 3 does *not* incorporate the common end cap and common inlet cap limitations, and therefore infringement of Claim 3 can be shown without establishing that the accused apparatus contains common end and inlet caps, or, for that matter, any end or inlet caps. An analogous reading applies to Claim 4.

Different scopes result when the same claim set is repeated but with different dependencies such that each claim depends from the claim immediately preceding it. The set will then read as follows:

1. Apparatus for injecting a reactive gas into a soil formation, comprising:

   an outer length of hollow tubing having a side wall with openings less than 200 microns in diameter; and an inner length of hollow tubing disposed within said outer length, said inner length having a side wall with openings less than 200 microns in diameter.

2. The apparatus of claim 1 further comprising a common end cap to seal the downstream ends of both lengths of hollow tubing and a common inlet cap with separate openings leading to the interior of said inner length of tubing and the annular space between said inner and outer lengths of tubing.
3. The apparatus of claim 2 further comprising porous packing material disposed in the annular space between said inner and outer lengths of tubing.
4. The apparatus of claim 3 wherein said inner and outer lengths of tubing are coaxial circular cylinders.

Here, the scope of Claim 3 has been narrowed relative to its earlier form to incorporate the limitations of both Claims 1 and 2, and is infringed only by an apparatus that contains inner and outer lengths of tubing, openings in the side walls of each with diameters not exceeding 200 microns, a common end cap for each length of tubing and a common inlet cap, plus porous packing material in the annular space. Claim 4 likewise incorporates the limitations of Claims 1, 2, and 3, further requiring that the inner and outer lengths of tubing be coaxial circular cylinders (as opposed, for example, to cylinders of elliptical or polygonal cross section, or cylinders whose axes are eccentric rather than coaxial).

Any invention has a variety of parameters that can be used in drafting dependent claims either by adding explicit reference to particular parameters or by imposing limitations on them such as particular shapes, materials, size ranges, operating conditions, and the like. Each dependent claim provides a fallback position in the event that the broader claim from which the dependent claim depends is declared invalid or unenforceable. Optimally, the strategy in selecting limitations to place in the dependent claims would be based on predictions of the parameters of the invention that are the most likely sources of vulnerability, or of the feature that the patent holder will have to rely on to defend the validity of the patent. It is not unusual for different points of novelty to be stressed at different times. The patent attorney in the initial preparation of the patent application may for example stress one feature as the point of novelty while counsel for the plaintiff patent holder years later

during infringement litigation may feel that a different feature offers a stronger response to a validity challenge raised by the defendant and not considered by the patent attorney. While it is often
possible to predict the challenges that can be raised, dependent
claims generally entail a considerable degree of guesswork since one
can rarely predict all of the challenges.

The more dependent claims, therefore, the greater the ability to
withstand challenges. The number of possibilities is almost end-
less, however, since the fallback positions of the dependent claims
can be drawn not only from large numbers of system parameters,
but also from combining parameters in different ways. To avoid
excessive repetition, the patent regulations allow *multiple dependent* claims, which are dependent claims written in alternate form
to depend from two or more claims. This is demonstrated in the
following set of claims which begins with the claim quoted above to
the process for upgrading petroleum distillation bottoms:

1. A process for upgrading petroleum distillation bottoms, comprising:

   (a.) combining said distillation bottoms with an aqueous liq-
        uid to form a dispersion;

   (b.) treating said dispersion by irradiation with ultrasound
        sufficient to convert components of said distillation bot-
        toms to lower-boiling species; and

   (c.) separating an organic phase from said dispersion thus
        treated.

2. The process of claim 1 performed as a batchwise process.

3. The process of claim 1 performed as a continuous process.

4. The process of claims 2 or 3 further comprising preheating said
   distillation bottoms to a temperature exceeding 150°C.

5. The process of claims 2 or 3 further comprising contacting said
   dispersion with a transition metal catalyst while treating said
   dispersion with ultrasound.

6. The process of claims 2 or 3 further comprising recovering an
   aqueous phase from said dispersion thus treated and recycling
   said aqueous phase to step (a).

Claim 4 in this set is treated as two separate claims—its scope is
defined by combining its own limitations *either* with those of

claim 2, or with those of claim 3 (and in both cases with claim 1 as well). The same is true for claims 5 and 6. The options to the patent holder are therefore exactly the same as if the claims 4, 5, and 6 were set forth as two claims each, to give a total of nine claims rather than six. There is no limit to the number of claims that can be referenced in a multiple dependent claim, and the referenced claims can be either independent, dependent, or both. The only restriction is that no multiple dependent claim can depend from another multiple dependent claim. The use of multiple dependencies therefore offers the patent attorney a shortcut to claim drafting without compromising the flexibility afforded by a large number of claims.

As demonstrated above, individual claims in a claim set serve their various purposes only when they differ among themselves in scope. Inventors drafting their own claims are often tempted to use dependent claims for purposes of emphasis rather than scope variation, with results similar to those of Claim Set A below.

Since fluorine, chlorine, bromine, and iodine are the *only* halogens (other than astatine, which is extremely rare) in the Periodic Table, the listing of these four halogens in Claim 2 of Claim Set A provides no change in scope relative to Claim 1. As a result, if the same method involving any one of these four halogens was in the

Claim Set A	*Claim Set B*
1. A method for treating a storage container to inhibit microbial infestation comprising fumigating said container with a halogen-containing gas other than astatine.	1. A method for treating a storage container to inhibit microbial infestation comprising fumigating said container with a halogen-containing gas other than astatine.
2. The method of claim 1 in which the halogen in said halogen-containing gas is either fluorine, chlorine, bromine, or iodine.	2. The method of claim 1 in which the halogen in said halogen-containing gas is fluorine.
	3. The method of claim 1 in which the halogen in said halogen-containing gas is chlorine.
	4. The method of claim 1 in which the halogen in said halogen-containing gas is bromine.
	5. The method of claim 1 in which the halogen in said halogen-containing gas is iodine.

public domain at the time of the invention, both claims of Claim Set A will fall. Claim Set B, in contrast, offers the options that are lacking in Claim Set A, despite appearing similar to Claim Set A in listing the halogens first generically and then individually. In Claim Set B, each claim differs in scope and each of the four dependent claims offers a separate strategic position for the patent holder to fall back on in the event that Claim 1 fails.

FURTHER INDICATORS OF CLAIM SCOPE: LEGAL TERMS

It is stated above that the longer the claim, the more limitations it has and hence the narrower its scope. While this is presented as a general principle, it results in fact from certain legal terms in the claims of a patent. Legal terms appear in every discipline of law, and while their meanings originate from usages outside the legal context, the law, through judicial use and a need to make fine but critical distinctions, assigns more specific meanings to these words that in some cases differ considerably from their meanings in common usage. In patent claims, the key legal terms are "a" or "an," "comprising," "consisting essentially of," "consisting of," "means for," and "a member selected from the group consisting of." Claim Sets C, D, and E at the end of this chapter illustrate the use of these terms and their legal meanings.

The difference between the legal terms "a" or "an" and their nonlegal use is that as legal terms "a" or "an" each mean "one or more." (As in conventional usage, of course, the legal meaning of "a" is the same as that of "an.") Claim Set C illustrates how the term "a" preceding an element can be broader than claims limited either to one such element or to more than one. In Claim 1 of the set, "a" precedes each of the first two elements, i.e., the nanotube and the fullerene molecule. Claim 7 calls for a "plurality" of fullerene molecules within "said nanotube." This is legally interpreted to be narrower in scope than Claim 1, since Claim 1 is interpreted to cover (a) devices in which all nanotubes contain a single fullerene, (b) devices containing one or more nanotubes with one fullerene each plus one or more nanotubes with two or more fullerenes each, and (c) devices in which all nanotubes contain two or more fullerenes, whereas the "plurality" language in Claim 7 requires that at least one nanotube contain more than one fullerene (thereby *eliminating* those where all nanotubes contain only one fullerene each). Claim 8 illustrates the same result with the "nanotube" element itself as a component of the nanoscale memory device, limiting itself to devices that contain more than one nanotube. Claim 8 also replaces "means for moving said nanotube..." with a "single means" for moving an entire plurality of nanotubes, indicating that the "means for moving..." language in Claim 1 itself covers both means for moving only one nanotube and a common means for moving more than one nanotube, a result analogous to that of the use of "a."

Almost as ubiquitous as "a" or "an" in patent claims, and similar in legal meaning, is the term "comprising." This term denotes that the components, steps, or elements that follow it must all be present in a composition, process, system, etc., to constitute infringement, but that these are the only components, steps, or elements whose presence is *required.* Infringement exists *regardless* of whether any other components, steps, or elements are present. Illustrations of the use of "comprising" and how its scope can be narrowed in successive claims are found in Claim Sets C and D. In Claim Set C, the word "comprising" appears in the preamble to Claim 1, followed by the recitations of a nanotube, a fullerene molecule, and an activator. Claim 6, by the use of the term "further comprising," adds a charged particle to the recited components, thereby covering only those nanoscale memory elements that include all four components, and excluding those that include the first three but lack the charged particle. Claim 6 is thus narrower than Claim 1. Similarly, Claim 9 is narrower than Claim 1 but in a different way, requiring the presence of an electric field–generating component in a location adjacent to the nanotube(s). In Claim Set D, the word "comprising" appears in the preamble to Claim 1, followed by the recitations of three process steps, "combining," "consolidating," and "densifying." Claim 2, again by the use of the term "further comprising," adds a milling step as an intervening process step between the "combining" and "consolidating" steps. Claim 2 is thus narrower than Claim 1 by requiring that all four steps be performed to constitute infringement: a process that lacks the milling step will fall within Claim 1 but not Claim 2. As a practical guide, therefore, one can substitute both of the words "requiring" and "regardless" for the term "comprising"—i.e., "requiring" the presence of the named elements "regardless" of the presence or absence of any unnamed elements.

The terms "consisting essentially of" and "consisting of" are alternatives to "comprising" when narrower scopes are intended. The "requiring" part of the "comprising" definition is carried into these two terms as well; the "regardless" part is not. When "consisting essentially of" is used, infringement in the presence of unnamed elements occurs only if the unnamed elements are present in no more than trace amounts or to such a limited degree that they do not affect the nature or quality of the product. When the word "consisting" is used by itself, infringement occurs only when the named elements are the *only* elements present. Claims 2, 3, and 4 of Claim Set E illustrate the use of all three terms (although as verbs in the present tense rather than present participles). Claim 2 limits the antimicrobial agent to one that includes (i.e., requires the presence of) a chlorinated diphenyl ether (a class of antimicrobial compounds), and may or may not also include (i.e., regardless of the presence or absence of) other antimicrobial compounds (of different classes) in any amount. Claim 3 limits the antimicrobial agent to one that includes a chlorinated diphenyl ether, but either no other antimicrobial compounds of other classes or only those that might be present for incidental reasons (as manufacturing impurities, for example) and not in sufficient quantity to add to the antimicrobial effect. Claim 4 limits the antimicrobial agent to a chlorinated diphenyl ether and does not cover compositions in which any other antimicrobial compounds are present, even in trace amounts.

The word "consisting" also appears as part of another phrase that has a specific legal meaning—"a member selected from the group consisting of." This phrase is used to introduce a list of items and denotes that any of the items recited in the list will meet the claim limitation. The list is known in patent law as a "Markush group" in reference to a judicial decision which first recognized the usage of the phrase and defined its meaning. Claim 5 of Claim Set E uses the phrase to limit the scope of the antimicrobial agent by requiring that the agent be "selected from the group consisting of" chlorinated diphenyl ethers and chlorinated diphenyl ureas (two distinct classes of antimicrobial compounds). This makes Claim 5 broader than Claim 2, since any compound that falls within the two classes combined will fall within the scope of Claim 5 while Claim 2 requires that a member of the chlorinated diphenyl ether class be present. The result is contrary to the result achieved when the term "comprising" is used: the more items in the list, the larger the Markush group and the greater the number of possibilities. The article "a" preceding the word "member" has the meaning and effect described above: infringement exists if as few as one of the items in the list is present as well as if both items in the list (or two or more for longer lists) are present. The last two items in the list will always be separated by the connector "and," but because of the inclusion of "a" before "member," one can readily remember the scope by substituting "and/or." Coincidentally, the article "a" also appears before "chlorinated diphenyl ether" and "chlorinated diphenyl urea," indicating that more than one of each class can be present and still infringe. Finally, a more descriptive term can be used in place of the word "member" with no change in result. Thus, if Claim 1 were rewritten to incorporate the limitations that appear in Claim 5, the first recited element could be "an antimicrobial agent selected from the group consisting of a chlorinated diphenyl ether and a chlorinated diphenyl urea."

A further phrase serving as an indicator of scope in a patent claim is "means for..." followed by a gerund reciting a function. This phrase is typically used to introduce one component of a multicomponent apparatus claim and defines the component in terms of the function it serves rather than its physical structure or composition. The scope of a "means for..." recitation depends on the supporting description in the specification of the patent (the text preceding the claims), and is legally defined as the structures, materials, or acts that are explicitly described in the specification as serving the recited function, and their equivalents. This is the only phrase in claim language, therefore, that expressly requires a reading of the specification to determine its scope, together with a knowledge of what is or is not an equivalent of the described features. An example of a "means for..." phrase appears in Claim 1 of Claim Set A. To ascertain the scope of "means for moving said nanotube relative to said fullerene molecule or vice versa," the specification is reviewed for its description of movement mechanisms. If the only example given in the specification is a pair of electrodes positioned to apply a voltage between the ends of the nanotube, only the use of electrodes and any other equivalent means of applying a voltage will result in infringement. If for example a voltage difference between the ends of the nanotube can also be achieved by a laser-induced electric current, the laser and the electrodes may be considered equivalents and both would be covered regardless of whether the use of a laser is disclosed in the specification. If it can be shown that the two are not equivalent, the laser usage would only be covered if it were explicitly mentioned in the specification. If movement can also be achieved by using the tip of an atomic force microscope to deform the nanotube, this is most likely not an equivalent since it does not involve the application of a voltage. The use of the microscope would therefore not be covered by the "means for . . . " claim unless it were explicitly mentioned in the specification.

The breadth of the "means for . . . " limitation in Claim 1 is made apparent by Claim 9 which, as a dependent claim, is necessarily of lesser scope. Assuming that the "means for . . . " limitation in Claim 1 covers both the electrode structure and the laser arrangement, Claim 9 is narrower by covering only the laser arrangement.

The foregoing is not an attempt to provide a comprehensive treatment of claim interpretation, since the subject is one that is continually explored and refined by the courts and the patent system as a whole. The patent specification, the state of the art, and the application papers that form the official record of the patent (which is on file at the United States Patent and Trademark Office and available to the public) have all, at one time or another, influenced a court's interpretation of a claim and hence the outcome of a lawsuit for patent infringement. Nevertheless, the claims are the focal point of the patent holder's rights, and the terms and phrases discussed above offer at least a preliminary guide to claim interpretation.

Claim Set C

1. A nanoscale memory device comprising:

   a nanotube;

   a fullerene molecule disposed within said nanotube; and

   means for moving said nanotube relative to said fullerene molecule or vice versa.

2. The nanoscale memory device of claim 1 wherein said nanotube is formed from a member selected from the group consisting of carbon, boron, nitrogen, and mixtures thereof.

3. The nanoscale memory device of claim 1 wherein said nanotube is a carbon nanotube.

4. The nanoscale memory device of claim 1 wherein said nanotube is charged.

5. The nanoscale memory device of claim 1 wherein said fullerene molecule is charged.

6. The nanoscale memory device of claim 1 further comprising a charged particle disposed within said fullerene molecule.

7. The nanoscale memory device of claim 1 comprising a plurality of said fullerene molecules disposed within said nanotube.

8. The nanoscale memory device of claim 1 comprising a plurality of said nanotubes, each having a fullerene molecule disposed therein, and a single said means for moving said plurality of said nanotubes relative to said fullerene molecules or vice versa.

9. The nanoscale memory device of claim 1 in which said means for moving said nanotube relative to said fullerene molecule or vice versa comprises a laser beam source arranged to induce an electric current across said nanotube.

Claim Set D

1. A process for the manufacture of a ceramic body of high strength and toughness, said process comprising:

   (a.) combining a nanocrystalline metal oxide with nanotubes to form a nanoparticle mixture;

   (b.) consolidating said nanoparticle mixture into a green body; and

   (c.) densifying said green body by sintering under elevated temperature and pressure.

2. The process of claim 1 further comprising milling said nanoparticle mixture by high-energy ball milling prior to step (b).

3. The process of claim 1 wherein said nanotubes are carbon nanotubes.

4. The process of claim 1 wherein said nanotubes are single-wall carbon nanotubes.

5. The process of claim 1 wherein said metal oxide is a member selected from the group consisting of aluminum oxide, titanium oxide, magnesium oxide, and cerium oxide.

6. The process of claim 1 wherein said metal oxide is aluminum oxide.

7. The process of claim 1 wherein said nanotubes constitute from about 1 to about 50 volume percent of said nanoparticle mixture.

8. The process of claim 1 wherein step (c) is performed in the presence of an electric field.

9. The process of claim 7 wherein said electric field is a pulsed dc electric field.

Claim Set E

1. A deodorant composition comprising:

    an antimicrobial agent;
    denatured ethanol;
    an anhydrous carrier; and
    a gelling agent.

2. The deodorant composition of claim 1 wherein said antimicrobial agent comprises a chlorinated diphenyl ether.

3. The deodorant composition of claim 1 wherein said antimicrobial agent consists essentially of a chlorinated diphenyl ether.

4. The deodorant composition of claim 1 wherein said antimicrobial agent consists of a chlorinated diphenyl ether.

5. The deodorant composition of claim 1 wherein said antimicrobial agent is a member selected from the group consisting of a chlorinated diphenyl ether and a chlorinated diphenyl urea.

6. The deodorant composition of claim 1 wherein said antimicrobial agent comprises a chlorinated diphenyl urea.

7. The deodorant composition of claims 2 or 6 further comprising a siloxane anti-cracking agent.

8. The deodorant composition of claims 2 or 6 wherein said antimicrobial agent constitutes from about 0.1% to about 5% by weight of said composition.

Chapter 4

Monopoly or Maze?
The Board Game Approach
to Claim Analyses

The claims of a patent offer the patent holder a legally sanctioned monopoly, but they also present an array of strategies when the patent contains a multitude of claims, as opposed to the rare patent with only a single claim. Claim sets offer strategies not only to the patent holder but also to investors and parties in general that are engaged in business relationships with the patent holder. Strategies to approaching the claims are also applied by infringers of the patent, by challengers of the validity of the patent, and even by the patent examiner while the application for patent is pending. With these strategies, the monopoly afforded by any single patent is multifaceted, and finding one's way through the claim set can itself present a challenge, particularly when a large number of claims are involved. Each party approaching the claims has a distinct purpose in mind, and often one that is unique to the particular party.

To help in selecting the appropriate approach, the claim set of a patent can be visualized as a two-dimensional diagram. Examples of such diagrams are presented in Figures 4.1, 4.2, and 4.3, each representing the full set of claims of a different (fictitious) patent.

In these diagrams, each claim appears as an enclosed area (rectangles are used for convenience) whose outline represents the boundaries of the scope of the claim as defined by the claim limitations. One of the critical characteristics of claims that the rectangular areas illustrate is that every dependent claim is narrower in scope than the claim that is referenced by the dependent claim, whether the referenced claim is an independent claim or another dependent claim. Thus, the rectangle representing a dependent claim resides

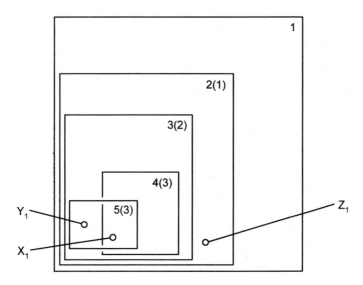

Figure 4.1. Claim Set as a Two-Dimensional Diagram: First Example

fully within the rectangle representing the claim that the dependent claim depends from. Another critical characteristic is that no two claims of any one patent are of the same scope. Thus, two rectangles may be of the same size, but no two rectangles are coextensive.

The geometrical arrangements of the rectangles signify the following claim structures.

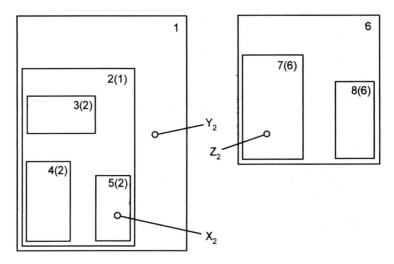

Figure 4.2. Claim Set as a Two-Dimensional Diagram: Second Example

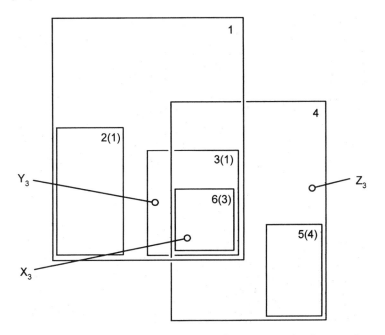

Figure 4.3. Claim Set as a Two-Dimensional Diagram: Third Example

The patent whose claim set is represented by Figure 4.1 has a total of five claims of which one is independent and four are dependent. The claim numbers are indicated in an upper corner of the rectangle representing each claim, with each dependent claim represented by a number followed by a second number in parentheses, the number in parentheses being that of the claim that the dependent claim depends from. Thus, claim 1 is independent, claim 2 depends from claim 1, claim 3 depends from claim 2, and claims 4 and 5 each depend from claim 3. Claim 1 thus has the most widely spaced boundaries and hence the broadest scope while each of the remaining claims is fully contained within the boundaries, and hence the scope, of claim 1, but each having its own, narrower boundaries. Anything falling within the scope of claim 2 thus also falls within the scope of claim 1; anything falling within claim 3 also falls within claims 1 and 2; and anything falling within either of claim 4 or claim 5 also falls within claims 1, 2, and 3. Using "device" claims as an illustration: device X_1 falls within all five claims; device Y_1 falls within claims 1, 2, 3, and 5 but not 4; and device Z_1 falls within claims 1 and 2 but not claims 3, 4, or 5.

Figure 4.2 represents the claim set of a patent that has a total of eight claims, two of which are independent and six are dependent.

The claim numbers and their dependencies are indicated in the same manner as those of Figure 4.1, and the analysis is the same as that of Figure 4.1 except that the eight claims in the patent reside in two groups, each containing one independent claim and two or more dependent claims. In the first set, claim 1 is independent, claim 2 depends from claim 1, and each of claims 3, 4, and 5 depends from claim 2. In the second set, claim 6 is the independent claim and each of claims 7 and 8 depends from claim 6. Device X_2 falls within claims 1, 2, and 5, but not claims 3, 4, 6, 7, or 8. Device Y_2 falls within claim 1 but within none of claims 2, 3, 4, 5, 6, 7, and 8. Device Z_2 falls within claims 6 and 7, but not claims 1, 2, 3, 4, 5, or 8.

The patent of Figure 4.3 has a greater degree of overlap among the claims, a situation more typical than those of Figures 4.1 and 4.2. This patent has a total of six claims of which two are independent and four are dependent, and the claim-numbering system of Figures 4.1 and 4.2 is used here as well. The two independent claims are claims 1 and 4, which overlap with each other but are written as independent claims. Overlapping independent claims are permitted by patent regulations provided they differ in scope. In this case, the two independent claims do indeed differ in scope, as indicated by their noncoextensive boundaries. Each of claims 2 and 3 depends from claim 1, as they must, since each has at least a portion that lies outside the boundary of claim 4. Claim 5 depends from claim 4, and claim 6 can depend either from claim 1, claim 3, or claim 4. In this case, claim 6 depends from claim 3. Device X_3 falls within claims 1, 3, 4, and 6 but not claim 2 or claim 5; device Y_3 falls within claims 1 and 3 but not claims 2, 4, 5, or 6; device Z_3 falls within claim 4 only.

Using these two-dimensional diagrams as mental images of claim sets, one can approach a claim set like a board game. Depending on the game, the "pieces" will be either infringing devices or pieces of prior art, and the choice of game is determined by the identity of the player and the goal sought by the player, i.e., the reason for the analysis. Five such "board games" are described below.

BOARD GAME NO. 1: "ARE THESE CLAIMS ALLOWABLE OVER THE PRIOR ART?"

The player of this game is a patent examiner examining an application for patent prior to issuing an "Office Action," i.e., an official statement indicating the examiner's findings as to the merits of the application. The board is the claim set of the patent application, and the goal is to perform a search of the prior art, and then to decide on the basis of the search whether to allow the claims and issue a patent on the application or to reject the claims for lack of novelty. The "pieces" in this game are thus disclosures in the prior art. A claim will lack novelty if the examiner finds a disclosure in the prior art (i.e., an actual device or a description of a device) that is encompassed by the claim. Novelty is only one of several criteria that the examiner will apply, but this example addresses only novelty. The patent applicant who understands this game will be able to understand the explanations provided by the Office Action and be better equipped to respond.

The examiner begins by searching the prior art for the subject matter of the narrowest claims, and selects those claims whose scopes fall within the scopes of all other claims of the patent. In the patent of Figure 4.1, the narrowest claims are claims 4 and 5, both of which are encompassed by claims 1, 2, and 3. The search seeks to find a prior art disclosure that falls within the boundaries of the rectangles representing both claims 4 and 5, or claims 4 and 5 individually. Any disclosure that falls within these boundaries also falls within those of the remaining three claims. If item X_1 is found by the search, the examiner will reject all five claims of the patent for lack of novelty. If the search does not reveal X_1 but instead reveals Y_1, only claims 1, 2, 3, and 5 will be rejected for lack of novelty, and claim 4 will be allowed, since Y_1 meets all the limitations of claim 5 but not all those of claim 4.

In the patent of Figure 4.2, the search may cover all eight claims, or only one of the two nonoverlapping sets. Here, the examiner must search for prior art that falls within claims 3, 4, 5, 7, and 8 to cover all eight claims. If claims 6 through 8 are set aside and claims 1 through 5 are searched first and the search reveals item X_2, claims 1, 2, and 5 will be rejected and claims 3 and 4 allowed. If the search reveals item Y_2 and not item X_2, only claim 1 will be rejected, while claims 2 through 5 will all be allowed. A similar analysis applies to claims 6, 7, and 8, where the search begins with claims 7 and 8.

The patent represented by Figure 4.3 offers a more complex board, but the approach is the same. If all six claims are being examined, the examiner will begin by focusing on the subject matter of claims 2, 5, and 6, since prior art within each of these claims must be found before all six claims can be rejected. If X_3 alone is found, claims 2 and 5 will be allowed, and these claims will still be allowed if the search produces X_3, Y_3, and Z_3. If Y_3 and Z_3 are found but not X_3, claim 6 will also be allowed. Results with other combinations are readily apparent.

BOARD GAME NO. 2: "ARE WE COVERED?"

The player in this board game is either the patent owner, a party seeking to make an investment in the patent holder, an industry member seeking to purchase the patent or to obtain licensing rights under the patent (particularly an exclusive license), an industry partner considering a joint venture with the patent holder, or an attorney performing due diligence on behalf of any of these parties. The analysis is performed either on an issued patent or on the claims of a pending application, and the goal is to confirm that a particular device of interest or a product line is covered by the patent. If the answer is positive, the player will know that the patent will serve its intended purpose of preventing competitors from entering the market for that device or product line. The "piece" in this game is therefore the device or product line.

The game is relatively simple since the goal is met by identifying, among all the claims of the patent, any claim whose limitations are met by the device or, in the case of a product line, at least one claim covering each device in the product line. The starting point of the game are the broadest claims, i.e., claim 1 of Figure 4.1, claims 1 and 6 of Figure 4.2, and claims 1 and 4 of Figure 4.3, since the widely spaced boundaries of these claims make them the easiest to meet. Coverage is stronger however when the device or product line also falls within one or more dependent claims, since these serve as back-up claims if the broader claims fail, and the narrower scope of the dependent claims makes them less vulnerable to challenge. Of course, the reasons why a product is developed for marketing are based on the product itself rather than the number of claims that cover it. At the drafting stage of the patent application, however, the claim set can be prepared with an awareness of the products for which the patent holder will specifically wish to have strong coverage.

The number of claims found to cover any single device and the breadth of each claim will have implications for the investor, purchaser, licensee, or joint venture partner as well, and these are reflected in the board games discussed below.

BOARD GAME NO. 3: "DO WE INFRINGE?"

The board in this board game is an issued patent rather than a patent application, and the player is a competitor of the patent holder who seeks to determine whether a device that the competitor proposes to market will subject the competitor to infringement liability under the patent. The inquiry in this case starts with the independent claims rather than the dependent claims, and asks whether the proposed device (the "piece" of the game) will meet all the limitations of the independent claims.

The game begins with the independent claims, since these will collectively encompass all claims of the patent. The broadest claims of the claim set will necessarily be independent claims, but many patents will also contain independent claims that are very narrow in scope. These must be included in this initial part of the analysis as well, since one can never be assured that a product falling outside the scope of a single independent claim will also fall outside the scope of other independent claims in the same patent, regardless of their scope. It is the independent nature of independent claims, rather than their broad or narrow scope, that requires them to be considered first.

If in the patent of Figure 4.1, the proposed device falls outside claim 1, the competitor can conclude that none of the claims will be infringed, since claims 2 through 5 are all within the scope of claim 1 and anything falling outside claim 1 will fall outside all five. Thus, if the comparison with claim 1 is successful from the competitor's perspective, the analysis can end with the study of only a single claim. The patent of Figure 4.2 receives the same approach, except that two independent claims (claims 1 and 6) are present rather than one. The analysis thus begins with the study of both claims 1 and 6. The proposed device is compared against these two claims individually, and if it falls within neither, none of the claims of the patent are infringed, and the analysis is complete after the study of two claims rather than the entire set of eight. The patent of Figure 4.3 receives the same type of analysis as that of Figure 4.2, focusing again on the independent claims, claims 1 and 4. Even though these two claims overlap, the comparison of the proposed device to claim 4 is still performed independently of the comparison to claim 1. Here again, if neither is met by the device, none of the claims of the patent are infringed.

If one or more independent claims cannot be dismissed in this manner, the player looks to the dependent claims that reference the infringed independent claims, and identifies all claims, independent and dependent, that will be infringed. The player then commences Board Game No. 4 for a further investigation into the question of infringement liability.

BOARD GAME NO. 4: "INVALIDATE THE CLAIM!"

As noted above, the player in this game is likewise a competitor of the patent holder, and the game is played after receiving an unfavorable result in Board Game No. 3. The player in Board Game No. 3 has thus been unable to conclude that the proposed device falls outside the scope of all of the independent claims of the patent and has identified certain claims that will be infringed. The player then seeks to establish that each of the infringed claims is invalid, and does so by searching the prior art for a device that falls within the scope of (legal term: "anticipates") each of those claims. The prior art device may be one that the player discovers through independent searching, or one that the player had itself published, made the subject of a commercial operation or transaction or otherwise placed in the public domain. The game thus potentially involves two devices or "pieces," one that the player proposes to market and one that is in the prior art. The latter "piece" serves to clear the former "piece" for liability-free marketing.

In the patent of Figure 4.1, the device proposed for marketing may for example be Z_1, falling within the scope of claims 1 and 2 but not 3, 4, or 5. Any prior art device falling within the scope of ("anticipating") claims 1 and 2 will invalidate both of these claims. Thus, if Z_1 itself is found in the prior art (i.e., the single device serving as both "pieces" of the game), both claims will be invalid. The same result will also be achieved however if either X_1 or Y_1 is found in the prior art (X_1 or Y_1 thereby serving as the prior art "piece" while Z_1 is the proposed device "piece"). If however the device proposed for marketing is X_1, which falls within the scope of all five claims, finding Y_1 in the prior art will succeed in clearing X_1 of infringement liability but finding Z_1 will not, since Z_1 will anticipate only claims 1 and 2, leaving claims 3, 4, and 5 standing. If the patent is that of Figure 4.3 and the device proposed for marketing is Y_3, which falls within claims 1 and 3, the device will be cleared of liability if X_3 is found in the prior art, since the claims that X_3 anticipates include claims 1 and 3. If only Z_3 is found in the prior art, Y_3 will not be cleared, since Z_3 anticipates only claim 4, leaving claims 3 and 6 standing.

BOARD GAME NO. 5: "STOP THE INFRINGER!"

The player in this game is the patent holder, and the opponent is a competitor who is marketing a device within the scope of the patent without a license or other authorization from the patent holder. The device being marketed is thus the "piece." The patent holder considers bringing suit against the infringing competitor, but understands that the course that any legal action will take and the final resolution of the action are both unpredictable, and that maintaining the action may entail large sums in legal fees and a long time before a final resolution is reached. The goal of the patent holder is therefore to enforce the patent at a minimum cost but with the best chance for success in prevailing over the infringer. Both the cost and the chances of success are determined by the types of challenge that the infringer will bring in defense, and patent litigation is particularly well known for the wide variety of challenges that the infringer can raise. Certain challenges are directly related to claim scope, and the level of risk to the patent holder, and hence in some measure the costs and chances of success, can be associated to some degree with claim scope. For challenges that are related to claim scope, therefore, as noted in Chapter 3, the narrower the claim, the lower the risk.

If the patent is that of Figure 4.1 and the infringing device is Z_1, the claims available to the patent holder are claims 1 and 2, since these are the only claims that cover Z_1. Claim 2 is preferable to claim 1, since the narrower scope of claim 2 makes this claim a lower risk. If the infringing device is Y_1, the patent holder has more options to choose from, since Y_1 is covered by claims 3 and 5, in addition to 1 and 2, and the narrower scopes of claims 3 and 5 make them successively less vulnerable to challenge and hence of lower risk. A still greater number of options is available when the infringing device is X_1, since this device falls within all five claims of the patent, and the defeat of any four will still leave one claim standing and infringed. Similar analyses can be applied to the patents of Figures 4.2 and 4.3.

The patent holder does not choose the infringing device, of course, and will typically be unable to predict, at any time when the claims can be modified, which devices will be brought to market that the patent holder will wish to enjoin, particularly since the infringing device may first appear years after the patent has issued. This "game," nevertheless, demonstrates the value of a patent with a number of claims of overlapping yet varying scope, including claims that are fully contained within other claims but smaller in scope, as in claims 1, 2, 3, and 4 of Figure 4.1, and those that overlap in part with each also extending to areas not covered by the other, as in claims 4 and 5 of Figure 4.1 and claims 3 and 4 of Figure 4.3. Typically, all infringed claims will be asserted, but those of narrower scope will serve as effective back-up positions when broader claims are successfully challenged. When narrow claims that cover the infringing device are present, the broader claims will not be challenged at all, since the challenge will serve no purpose.

CONCLUSION

The avid fan of board games who seeks to construct a diagram corresponding to those of Figures 4.1, 4.2, and 4.3 for an actual patent will discover that this is a difficult task, particularly with the claim sets that one typically finds in technology patents. The diagrams are best treated as generalized mental images, and the "games" are best understood as metaphors for approaching the particular questions or goals that are quoted above as the game titles. The principal purpose of these analogies is to demonstrate approaches to independent and dependent claims in each of the various scenarios that will provide a complete answer in a manner consistent with the legalities of claim interpretation and without undue effort or excessive repetition.

Chapter 5

Identifying Prior Art: The First Step in Determining Patentability

If the claims are the playing field for strategies in both the enforcement of a patent and attacks on the validity of the patent, the "prior art" is the playing field for the invention itself and the determination of its patentability. Any discovery or innovation can advance the state of the art, and some by their nature can even present the discoverer or innovator with a proprietary position. To qualify as a patentable invention, however, the discovery or innovation must first meet a set of legal standards collectively referred to as patentable novelty. Novelty is the threshold of patentability and is defined relative to the "prior art." One must first therefore be able to identify the prior art.

A practical definition of "prior art" is anything that can be raised against a patent claim to deprive the invention in that claim of patentable novelty. Knowing what is or is not prior art is not intuitive, however, since it reflects more than the simple notion of whether anyone has ever seen, heard, or thought of the invention before the one who is applying for a patent. Identifying prior art is in fact one of the aspects of the patent system that reflect efforts to accommodate a variety of interests and public policies that tend to conflict with each other. The legally sanctioned monopoly conferred by a patent, for example, can be viewed as contradictory to the general public policy of promoting competition in the marketplace. Competition is generally recognized as a means of increasing efficiency, optimization, and economic benefit for the general welfare, and expressions of pro-competition public policy can be found in various statutes and legal doctrines whose purpose is to discourage or prohibit monopolies. Nevertheless, the interest in encouraging and promoting innovation by rewarding the innovator with a limited monopoly can be as strong as the interest in promoting competition.

The legal parameters defining prior art are an attempt to accommodate these and other interests. While the parameters are complex, a rudimentary understanding is of considerable value since the ability to identify prior art can be a decisive factor in decisions made by the patent holder and by competitors and partners of the patent holder. The patent holder, for example, will often be confronted with a need to defend its patents or to assess their viability relative to the prior art. This can arise at an early stage, when, for instance, the chances of obtaining a patent are weighed against the cost of the patent application or potential revenue from the patent. The need can also arise at a late stage such as after the patent has been granted, when the strength of the patent is weighed against the cost of enforcement and possible litigation. Likewise, one who receives a threatening notice from the patent holder or who independently discovers a patent that appears to block one's commercial activities, will conduct a prior art review to determine whether a challenge to the novelty of the patent can be made and whether the cost of the challenge is justified by its chance of success. These concerns are present in any due diligence review since they affect both freedom to operate and the viability of one's own patents.

The identification of prior art generally entails a consideration of four factors: category, timing, geography, and jurisdiction. The category factor asks whether a particular form of activity qualifies as prior art; the timing factor asks whether the "effective date" of the activity is early enough to qualify the activity as prior art; the geographical factor asks in what geographical location the activity occurred; and the jurisdictional factor looks to the legal system of the particular country or multinational region where the patent has been granted to determine the parameters that are applicable to a determination of prior art in that country or region. The term "activity" herein denotes both physical activity and expressive activity (verbal or other conveyances of information) that might qualify as prior art. In the following discussion, the prior art is arranged by category, with explanations of the remaining factors included within each category.

PRIOR ART BY CATEGORY

As the range of categories will demonstrate, prior art can be found in the activities of the inventor, the activities of the patent holder (typically the inventor's employer), and the activities of the challenger to the patent, as well as the activities of those who have no involvement with or interest in the patent at all. This discussion focuses on prior art relative to U.S. patents; in other jurisdictions, certain differences appear, the most prominent being in determination of the effective date and how prior art is applied and can be overcome.

The categories of prior art are (1) patents and patent-related documents, including various forms of published applications, (2) published materials other than patents, (3) business or commercial activities, transactions, and communications, and (4) oral disclosures.

Patents and Patent-related Documents

Patents and patent applications become prior art upon publication, and when publication occurs in stages, such as the publication of a pending application followed by the publication of the patent, or the publication of a patent followed by the publication of a reissue of the patent, prior art status attaches at the earliest publication. The category referred to herein as "patents and patent-related documents" includes issued patents, published patent applications (also referred to as "pre-grant patent publications"), defensive publications, statutory invention registrations, and any patents or patent applications published by a patent authority anywhere in the world, including documents similar to patents such as utility models, patents of addition, and the like. Among the patents granted by the United States Patent and Trademark Office (USPTO) are utility patents (i.e., those directed to the functional features of an invention), design patents, and plant patents.

An issued patent can be prior art regardless of whether or not the patent is in force. Prior art thus includes patents that are within their terms as well as patents that are expired, invalid (whether or not declared so in litigation), withdrawn, re-filed, or re-issued. A pre-grant patent publication can be prior art regardless of whether it later matures into an issued patent or is abandoned subsequent to its publication, and regardless of whether it was amended after publication or left unchanged. Both patents and published patent applications can be prior art regardless of where they were applied for, in which jurisdiction they were issued or published, or the language in which they were published.

Chapters 3 and 4 emphasize the significance of the claims of a patent and the rights and strategies that they afford the patent applicant and patent holder. When a patent is viewed as prior art, however, the claims generally have no significance. Any portion of the patent (or patent-related document), including those portions that are not related to what the patent or application claims as its own invention, has as much prior art value as any other portion. The specification, i.e., the portion of the text of the patent other than its claims and its abstract, is nevertheless the most important portion, since all recitations in the claims must appear in the text of the patent as well, and the text is typically more descriptive than the claims. Discussions of the background of the invention are thus of relevance, as are any comparative descriptions such as discussions of any differences between the invention and its alternatives and any test data that are included to demonstrate the improvement that the invention offers.

In addition to the specification, the entire official record of the patent or application that is on file with the patent authorities to whom the application was submitted becomes prior art when the patent is issued or the application published. This official record is commonly referred to as the "file history," and in most cases does not contain anything of value that is not also present in the patent or published application. In some cases, however, the file history contains additional statements or documents that were submitted by the inventor's attorney as part of an argument made to the examiner. These may have value on their own as prior art.

The effective date of a patent, pre-grant publication, or any other patent-related document varies with the jurisdiction that published the document. For patents and pre-grant publications published by the USPTO, the effective date is the filing date of the application of which the document is the published form. For publications that cite two or more filing dates, the effective date is the earliest of those cited, with two exceptions (explained below). For documents in the file history of a U.S. patent or pre-grant publication, the effective date is the date on which the patent was issued or the pre-grant publication published. For patents and patent applications published by patent jurisdictions other than the United States, the effective date is the publication date, or in cases where the document was published more than once, the earliest publication date.

Patent-related documents published in the United States that list two or more filing dates reflect the practice of filing a patent application with a claim for a "related" status or a "priority" status which affords a later application a certain benefit of the filing date of an earlier application. This practice, which is explained in Chapter 9 of this book, may involve the claiming of a filing date benefit from another U.S. patent application, from an international patent application filed under the Patent Cooperation Treaty (PCT), from a foreign patent application that is cited as a "priority" document, or from any number or combination of these applications. When one or more earlier filed U.S. applications are listed, the listing will state for each application other than the first filed that the application is "related" to its predecessor(s) as a "continuation," a "continuation-in-part," or a "division," or that the earlier filed is a "provisional" application of which the later filed is a "nonprovisional." In each case, the effective date is the earliest of the filing dates listed. The first of two exceptions resides in the listing of a "foreign application priority" document: the filing date of the foreign application does not serve as an effective date of the U.S. document for prior art purposes. The second exception arises when the portion of the specification that is relevant as prior art in the later filed application is not present in the earlier filed application. This can occur when the later application is a "continuation-in-part" of the earlier application, or when the relation between the two documents is that of "provisional" and "nonprovisional." The specification of a "continuation-in-part" typically contains material that is not present in the earlier ("parent") application, hence the "in-part" portion of the term, and the specification of a provisional application is often expanded when resubmitted as nonprovisional application. In both cases, therefore, the earlier application itself must be examined to determine whether its filing date is also the effective filing date of the published document for the portion of the published document that has value as prior art.

Figures 5.1 through 5.11 illustrate the various date listings and how they appear on patents, pre-grant publications, and other patent-related documents. Each figure shows the cover page of the document, as shown below.

By international convention, the data shown on the cover page of each document are indexed by a standardized indexing system that

Figure No.	*Cover Page of*
5.1	U.S. Pre-Grant Publication
5.2	U.S. Pre-Grant Publication
5.3	U.S. Patent
5.4	U.S. Defensive Publication
5.5	U.S. Statutory Invention Registration
5.6	U.S. Design Patent
5.7	Published International (PCT) Patent Application
5.8	Published European Patent Application
5.9	Published Japanese Patent Application (*Kokai*)
5.10	Granted Japanese Patent (*Kokoku*)
5.11	Published Chinese Patent Application

appears as numbers in parentheses (or in some cases, brackets or circles) that precede the data. This indexing system, established by the World Intellectual Property Organization, is known as the "Internationally Agreed Upon Numbers for the Identification of Bibliographic Data" and the acronym INID. For documents that are not in a language understood by the reader, the system facilitates the identification of a particular datum. Some of these index numbers and the data they represent are listed below.

Figure 5.1 is the cover page of a published U.S. patent application. The publication number appears in the upper right corner as item (10), and the number assigned to the application upon its filing is shown in the left column as item (21). Two dates appear on the sheet: the publication date, appearing as item (43), and the application filing date, appearing as item (22). The effective date of this document is its filing date.

Index	*Datum*
(10)	U.S. Publication No. (Patent or Application)
(11)	Non-U.S. Publication No. (Patent or Application)
(21)	Application No.
(22)	Application Filing Date
(30)	Priority Data from Application Filed in Another Jurisdiction
(43)	Date of Publication of Application Prior to Examination
(45)	Date of Patent
(62)	Data Regarding Related, Earlier-Filed Application(s)

US 20040093222A1

(19) **United States**
(12) **Patent Application Publication** (10) Pub. No.: **US 2004/0093222 A1**
Sipe et al. (43) **Pub. Date:** **May 13, 2004**

(54) **METHOD AND SYSTEM FOR ADDRESS INFORMATION DISTRIBUTION**

(76) Inventors: **Wayne Sipe**, Mansfield, TX (US); **Ben F. Bruce,** Arlington, TX (US); **Shahrom Kiani,** Arlington, TX (US); **Alan E. O'Martin,** Coppell, TX (US); **Gary Allen,** Arlington, TX (US); **John J. Mampe,** Fort Worth, TX (US)

Correspondence Address:
Philip G. Meyers Law Office
Suite 302
1009 Long Prairie Road
Flower Mound, TX 75022 (US)

(21) Appl. No.: **10/290,029**

(22) Filed: **Nov. 7, 2002**

Publication Classification

(51) Int. Cl.^{7} G06F 17/60; G06F 17/00
(52) U.S. Cl. 705/1; 705/404

(57) **ABSTRACT**

A process according to the invention takes daily address information and uses it to update the United States Postal Service (USPS) NCOA database, creating a new database that is current daily. The new database will assist businesses in making corrections to address information prior to printing address labels and delivering the items to a mail or parcel service provider. This process will enable the collection of address change information at near real time, validate the change information, and distribute this new database to licensed users on a daily or more frequent basis.

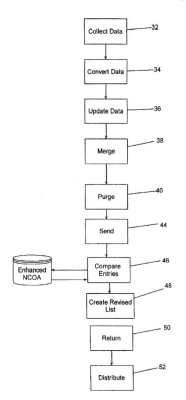

Figure 5.1. U.S. Pre-Grant Publication, Cover Page: First Example

Figure 5.2 is the cover page of another published U.S. patent application. This page differs from that of Figure 5.1 by listing three filing dates. The application represents the U.S. phase of an international application filed under the PCT, and both the number assigned to the application by the PCT Receiving Office and the number assigned by the USPTO appear in the left column, as items (86) and (21), respectively. None of the filing dates listed are the actual U.S. filing date, since under the provisions of the Treaty the PCT filing date is recognized as the U.S. filing date. The date shown as item (22) is therefore the PCT filing date. The second and third filing dates are listed under the "Foreign Application Priority Data" heading (item (30)). These dates are the filing dates for each of the two foreign patent applications (both filed in Great Britain) for which foreign priority is claimed. Neither of these serves as the effective date of this document; the effective date is the PCT filing date.

Figure 5.3 is the cover page of a U.S. patent. The filing date of the application on which the patent issued is indicated as item (22), and the number and filing date of a "related" application are shown in the "Related U.S. Application Data" which appears as item (62). Assuming that the relevant portions of the description in the document also appear in the related application, as is typically the case where as here the later application is a "division" of the earlier, the effective filing date is that of the earlier application. The cover page also lists, under item (56) "References Cited," a series of documents that were prior art relative to the patent itself, and among these are a series of U.S. patent documents. The dates cited for the various patents in the list are the issue dates of the patents rather than their filing dates or any effective dates that may differ from the filing dates. With regard to the document that is shown, however, and its status as prior art, the information in the "References Cited" list is not relevant.

The U.S. defensive publication, illustrated by the example of Figure 5.4, is one of the less common patent-related publications, although still citing several dates in addition to its publication date. The 1976 filing date of the application on which this publication was based is listed as item [22], and two earlier applications, filed in 1975 and 1973, respectively, are listed as "related" applications, with particulars listed as item [63]. Since the 1976 application was a "continuation" of the 1975 application, and the latter was a continuation of the 1973 application, all three are likely to have identical specifications, and any relevant portions of the document shown are likely to appear as well in the 1973 application. The

US 20040094567A1

(19) **United States**
(12) **Patent Application Publication** (10) Pub. No.: **US 2004/0094567 A1**
Pollock et al. (43) **Pub. Date:** **May 20, 2004**

(54) **TABLET DISPENSER FOR DISPENSING INDIVIDUAL TABLETS**

(76) Inventors: **Neil Pollock,** Melbourne Science Park Cambridge (GB); **Gary Sinclair,** New Market Suffolk (GB); **Paul Crossman,** Cambridgeshire (GB); **Andrian Caroen,** London (GB)

Correspondence Address:
Paul D Greeley
Ohlandt Greeley Ruggiero & Perle
9th Floor
One Landmark Square
Stamford, CT 06901-2682 (US)

(21) Appl. No.: **10/399,086**

(22) PCT Filed: **Oct. 12, 2001**

(86) PCT No.: **PCT/GB01/04560**

(30) **Foreign Application Priority Data**

Oct. 13, 2000 (GB) 0025110.8

Apr. 6, 2001 (GB) 0108743.6

Publication Classification

(51) **Int. Cl.[7]** **B65H 3/30**
(52) **U.S. Cl.** **221/289**

(57) **ABSTRACT**

According to the present invention there is provided a dispenser comprising (i) a container body **(10)**, (ii) a storage region **(12)** which is disposed within the container body **(10)** and which in use contains a multiplicity of items (C) to be individually dispensed, (iii) a dispensing outlet **(14)**, (iv) a passage between the storage region **(12)** and the dispensing outlet **(14)**, (v) a valve member **(38)** disposed between said storage region **(12)** and said outlet **(14)** moveable between an open position and a closed position, (vi) a stop member **(117)** spaced from said valve member **(38)** so as to define a passage region **(24)** of a size to accommodate an item (C) to be dispensed, said stop member **(117)** being moveable into and out of a closed position in which it prevents passage of an item (C) through said passage region **(24)**, and (vii) manually operable means **(34)** for moving said valve member **(38)** and said stop member **(117)**.

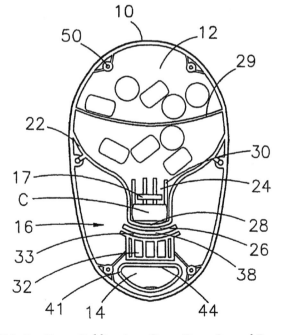

Figure 5.2. U.S. Pre-Grant Publication, Cover Page: Second Example

US006521447B2

(12) **United States Patent**

Zou et al.

(10) Patent No.: **US 6,521,447 B2**

(45) Date of Patent: **Feb. 18, 2003**

(54) **MINIATURIZED THERMAL CYCLER**

(75) Inventors: **Quanbo Zou**, Singapore (SG); **Uppili Sridhar**, Singapore (SG); **Yu Chen**, Singapore (SG); **Tit Meng Lim**, Singapore (SG); **Emmanuel Selvanayagam Zachariah**, Singapore (SG); **Tie Yan**, Singapore (SG)

(73) Assignee: **Institute of Microelectronics**, Singapore (SG)

(*) Notice: Subject to any disclaimer, the term of this patent is extended or adjusted under 35 U.S.C. 154(b) by 0 days.

(21) Appl. No.: **10/188,641**

(22) Filed: **Jul. 3, 2002**

(65) **Prior Publication Data**

US 2002/0173032 A1 Nov. 21, 2002

Related U.S. Application Data

(62) Division of application No. 09/785,588, filed on Feb. 16, 2001, now Pat. No. 6,432,695.

(51) Int. Cl.[7] C12M 1/34
(52) U.S. Cl. **435/287.2**; 435/288.4; 422/109
(58) Field of Search 435/286.1, 287.2, 435/287.3, 288.3, 288.4, 289.1, 303.1, 305.2; 422/102, 109, 113, 131; 216/2

(56) **References Cited**

U.S. PATENT DOCUMENTS

5,589,136 A	12/1996	Northrup et al.	422/102
5,639,423 A	6/1997	Northrup et al.	122/50
5,646,039 A	7/1997	Northrup et al.	435/287.2
5,674,742 A	10/1997	Northrup et al.	435/286.5
5,716,842 A	2/1998	Baier et al.	435/283.1
5,939,312 A	8/1999	Baier et al.	435/287.2
6,379,929 B1 *	4/2002	Buns et al.	435/91.2

OTHER PUBLICATIONS

Adam T. Woolley et al., (UC Berkeley), "Functional Integration of PCR Amplification and Capillary Electrophoresis in a Microfabricated DNA Analysis Device", Analytical Chem., vol. 68, pp. 4081–4086.
M. Allen Northrup, et al., (Lawrence Livermore Nat.'l Lab, UC Berkeley, Roche Molecular Systems), "DNA Amplification with a Microfabricated Reaction Chamber", 7th Int'l. Conf. Solid–State Sensors and Actuators, pp. 924–926.
Sundaresh N. Brahmasandra, et al., (U. Michigan), "On–Chip DNA Band Detection in Microfabricated Separation Systems", SPIE Conf. Microfluidic Devices and Systems, Santa Clara, CA, Sep. 1998, SPIE vol. 3515, pp. 242–251.

(List continued on next page.)

Primary Examiner—David A. Redding
(74) Attorney, Agent, or Firm—George O. Saile; Stephen B. Ackerman

(57) **ABSTRACT**

The invention describes a thermal cycler which permits simultaneous treatment of multiple individual samples in independent thermal protocols, so as to implement large numbers of DNA experiments simultaneously in a short time. The chamber is thermally isolated from its surroundings, heat flow in and out of the unit being limited to one or two specific heat transfer areas. All heating elements are located within these transfer areas and at least one temperature sensor per heating element is positioned close by. Fluid bearing channels that facilitate sending fluid into, and removing fluid from, the chamber are provided. The chambers may be manufactured as integrated arrays to form similar cycler chamber has independent temperature and fluid flow control. Two embodiments of the invention are described together with a process for manufacturing them.

27 Claims, 8 Drawing Sheets

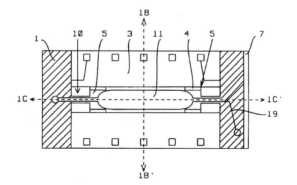

Figure 5.3. U.S. Patent, Cover Page

United States Defensive Publication [19] (H) [11] T954,006

Lee et al.

[43] **Jan. 4, 1977**

[54] **ON-CHIP SUBSTRATE VOLTAGE GENERATOR**

[75] Inventors: **James M. Lee**, Wappingers Falls; **George Sonoda**, Poughkeepsie, both of N.Y.

[73] Assignee: **International Business Machines**, Armonk, N.Y.

[21] Appl. No.: **672,898**

[22] Filed: **Apr. 2, 1976**

Related U.S. Application Data

[63] Continuation of Ser. No. 567,213, April 11, 1975, abandoned, which is a continuation of Ser. No. 375,271, June 29, 1973, abandoned.

[51] Int. Cl.² H03K 3/353
[52] U.S. Cl. 307/304; 357/41; 331/57

[57] **ABSTRACT**

Disclosed is an apparatus for generating and controlling a desired substrate potential level or a semiconductor chip. A pulse source, such as an oscillator, provides a pulse train which, in combination with a control signal from the substrate voltage detector, selectively discharges a capacitor in a voltage level converter for obtaining a desired level of substrate potential. A feedback path through the substrate regulates the conductivity of a reference transistor in the substrate voltage detector providing the required control signal.

1 Claim, 3 Sheets Drawing, 17 Pages Specification

The file of this unexamined application may be inspected and copies thereof may be purchased (849 O.G. 1221, Apr. 9, 1968).

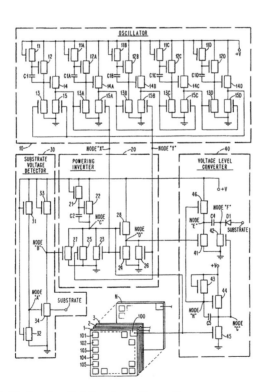

Figure 5.4. U.S. Defensive Publication, Cover Page

63

effective date is therefore the 1973 date, which is the earliest of the three.

Defensive publications were issued at the request of the applicant as a means of giving the contents of the publication the status of prior art. The issuance of defensive publications was discontinued after 1986, when they were replaced by statutory invention registrations, which bear many of the characteristics of defensive publications and are likewise issued at the request of the applicant. An example of a statutory invention registration is shown in Figure 5.5. The information shown on the cover page of this document is analogous to that of a patent or pre-grant publication. In this case, only one filing date is shown, again as item (22), which is also the effective date of this document as prior art.

Figures 5.1 through 5.5 are examples of utility patents and documents related to utility patents. The design patent represented by Figure 5.6 has a cover page with information similar to that of a utility patent, including its filing date which is listed as item [22]. While a design patent focuses on the ornamental features or appearance of the article shown in the figures of the patent, the figures may also indicate or suggest functional utility. If they do, the patent may be effective as prior art relative to a utility patent. As in all U.S. patents and patent-related documents, the filing date of a design patent is its effective date as prior art. These figures do not include a plant patent since plant patents do not disclose, depict, or suggest functionality and therefore will not serve as prior art relative to the claims of a utility patent.

The published international application whose cover page is shown in Figure 5.7 is the published version of a PCT application, which is a preliminary stage for filing a single patent application in a multitude of countries or geographical regions throughout the world, as explained in Chapter 9 of this book. While the published PCT application lists a variety of numbers and dates, the only date that serves as an effective date of this document as prior art is the international publication date, listed as item (43).

It will be noted that the "Priority Data" (item (30)) lists a number corresponding to a U.S. provisional patent application, together with the filing date of the provisional application. This indicates that the PCT application claims the benefit of the filing date of the provisional application. Even though the provisional application was filed in the United States, however, its filing date is not an effective date for the PCT application as prior art, since the PCT

US000001999B1

(19) **United States**

(12) **Statutory Invention Registration**
Newill et al.

(10) Reg. No.: **US H1999 H**
(43) **Published:** **Nov. 6, 2001**

(54) **TUNING SABOTED PROJECTILE PERFORMANCE THROUGH BOURRELET MODIFICATION**

(75) Inventors: **James F. Newill**, Landenberg, PA (US); **Christopher P. R. Hoppel**, Havre de Grace; **William H. Drysdale**, Aberdeen, both of MD (US)

(73) Assignee: **The United States of America as represented by the Secretary of the Army**, Washington, DC (US)

(21) Appl. No.: **09/261,761**

(22) Filed: **Mar. 3, 1999**

(51) Int. Cl.[7] **F42B 14/06**
(52) U.S. Cl. **102/521**
(58) Field of Search 102/520–523

(56) **References Cited**

U.S. PATENT DOCUMENTS

H165	*	11/1986	Silsby	102/520
H1412	*	2/1995	Kline et al.	102/521
2,998,780	*	9/1961	Anspacher et al.	102/523
4,187,783	*	2/1980	Campoli et al.	102/520
4,326,464	*	4/1982	Price	102/523
4,408,538	*	10/1983	Deffayet et al.	102/522
4,941,244	*	7/1990	Ortmann et al.	102/521
5,025,731	*	6/1991	Meyer et al.	102/521
5,103,735	*	4/1992	Kaste et al.	102/521
5,196,650	*	3/1993	Cutron	102/521
5,313,889	*	5/1994	Wilkerson et al.	102/521

FOREIGN PATENT DOCUMENTS

3904626	*	8/1990	(DE)	102/521
86711	*	8/1983	(EP)	102/521
3704027	*	8/1988	(EP)	102/521
417012	*	3/1991	(EP)	102/521

* cited by examiner

Primary Examiner—Harold J. Tudor
(74) *Attorney, Agent, or Firm*—Paul S. Clohan, Jr.

(57) **ABSTRACT**

Kinetic energy projectiles including sabots having stiffened bourrelets which tune and improve shot performance. Shot dispersion for the projectiles is decreased by reducing adverse dynamic perturbations imparted to the projectiles during projectile launch. Reducing dynamic perturbations is accomplished by better controlling interior ballistics by changing the stiffness of the sabot bourrelets.

33 Claims, 12 Drawing Sheets

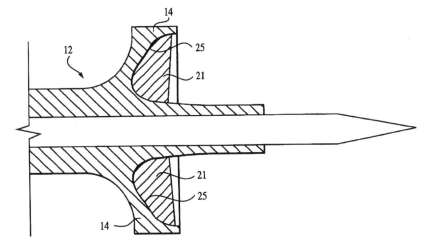

Figure 5.5. U.S. Statutory Invention Registration, Cover Page

United States Patent [19]

Duquaine, Jr. et al.

[11] Patent Number: **Des. 345,678**

[45] Date of Patent: ** Apr. 5, 1994

[54] **VEGETABLE SPINNER**

[75] Inventors: **Edward J. Duquaine, Jr.**, West Bend, Wis.; **William C. Cesaroni**, Glenview, Ill.

[73] Assignee: **The West Bend Company**, West Bend, Wis.

[**] Term: **14 Years**

[21] Appl. No.: **924,866**

[22] Filed: **Aug. 4, 1992**
[52] U.S. Cl. **D7/665**
[58] Field of Search D7/665, 667, 668; 34/8, 34/58; 99/479, 485, 495; 210/360.1

[56] **References Cited**

U.S. PATENT DOCUMENTS

D. 241,495	9/1976	Mantelet	D7/665
D. 257,203	10/1980	Doyel	D7/665
D. 328,551	8/1992	Kong	D7/665

Primary Examiner—Terry A. Wallace
Attorney, Agent, or Firm—Jansson & Shupe, Ltd.

[57] **CLAIM**

The ornamental design for a vegetable spinner, as shown and described.

DESCRIPTION

FIG. 1 is perspective view of a vegetable spinner showing our new design;
FIG. 2 is a side view, the opposite side being the miror image thereof;
FIG. 3 is a top plan view thereof; and,
FIG. 4 is a bottom plan view thereof.

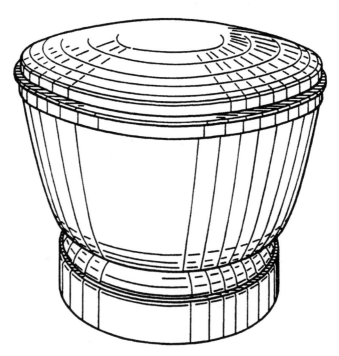

Figure 5.6. U.S. Design Patent, Cover Page

PCT   WORLD INTELLECTUAL PROPERTY ORGANIZATION
International Bureau

INTERNATIONAL APPLICATION PUBLISHED UNDER THE PATENT COOPERATION TREATY (PCT)

(51) International Patent Classification ^{7} :		(11) International Publication Number:	**WO 00/17675**
G02B 1/04, B29D 11/00, G02C 7/02, C08F 291/00	**A1**	(43) International Publication Date:	30 March 2000 (30.03.00)

<table>
<tr>
<td>

(21) International Application Number: PCT/US99/22048

(22) International Filing Date: 22 September 1999 (22.09.99)

(30) Priority Data:
 60/101,285   22 September 1998 (22.09.98)   US

(71) Applicant *(for all designated States except US)*: ZMS, LLC [US/US]; 5764 Shellmound Street, Emeryville, CA 94608 (US).

(72) Inventors; and
(75) Inventors/Applicants *(for US only)*: SOANE, David, S. [US/US]; 109 King Avenue, Piedmont, CA 94610 (US). HOUSTON, Michael [US/US]; 1429 Martin Luther King Jr. Way #E, Berkeley, CA 94709 (US). HINO, Toshiaki [JP/US]; Apartment 109, 1786 Spruce Street, Berkeley, CA 94709 (US).

(74) Agent: LARSON, Jacqueline, S.; Law Office of Jacqueline S. Larson, P.O. Box 2426, Santa Clara, CA 95055–2426 (US).

</td>
<td>

(81) Designated States: AE, AL, AM, AT, AU, AZ, BA, BB, BG, BR, BY, CA, CH, CN, CU, CZ, DE, DK, EE, ES, FI, GB, GD, GE, GH, GM, HR, HU, ID, IL, IN, IS, JP, KE, KG, KP, KR, KZ, LC, LK, LR, LS, LT, LU, LV, MD, MG, MK, MN, MW, MX, NO, NZ, PL, PT, RO, RU, SD, SE, SG, SI, SK, SL, TJ, TM, TR, TT, UA, UG, US, UZ, VN, YU, ZA, ZW, ARIPO patent (GH, GM, KE, LS, MW, SD, SL, SZ, TZ, UG, ZW), Eurasian patent (AM, AZ, BY, KG, KZ, MD, RU, TJ, TM), European patent (AT, BE, CH, CY, DE, DK, ES, FI, FR, GB, GR, IE, IT, LU, MC, NL, PT, SE), OAPI patent (BF, BJ, CF, CG, CI, CM, GA, GN, GW, ML, MR, NE, SN, TD, TG).

Published
With international search report.
Before the expiration of the time limit for amending the claims and to be republished in the event of the receipt of amendments.

</td>
</tr>
</table>

(54) Title: NEAR–NET–SHAPE POLYMERIZATION PROCESS AND MATERIALS SUITABLE FOR USE THEREWITH

(57) Abstract

This disclosure describes a processing approach for the rapid and efficient in–situ polymerization of specially prepared precursor mixtures to achieve near–net–shape production of objects/articles with exact dimensions. The process relies on the use of polymerizable compositions comprised of a mixture of a dead polymer, a reactive plasticizer and an initiator, which compositions are semi–solid–like and induce low shrinkage upon curing as a result of their partially polymerized nature prior to processing. The partially polymerized nature of the precursor mixtures also allows extremely impact–resistant objects/articles to be fabricated. Other desirable engineering property attributes can similarly be achieved via the judicious blending of starting ingredients in formulating the polymerizable (curable) mixtures.

Figure 5.7. Published International (PCT) Patent Application, Cover Page

application is an international document rather than a U.S. document. The same filing date may indeed be the effective date of a U.S. document that cites the provisional application under "Related U.S. Application Data," but only if that document is itself presented as prior art. Thus, if both a U.S. utility patent (or published application) and a published PCT application exist, both stemming from the same U.S. provisional application, the provisional application filing date will be an effective date only for the U.S. document.

Figure 5.8 is the cover page of a published European patent application. This page likewise shows a variety of numbers and dates. Among the dates are five priority dates (item (30)), a date of filing (item (22)), and a date of publication (item (43)). Since this is not a U.S. patent or patent-related document, the effective date of the document as prior art is the date of publication (item (43)).

The published Japanese patent application (*Kokai*) whose cover page is shown in Figure 5.9 similarly shows a series of numbers and dates, the dates including a filing date (item ㉒) and a date of publication (item ㊸). As in the published European patent application of Figure 5.7, the effective date is the date of publication.

The Japanese patent (*Kokoku*) whose cover page appears as Figure 5.10 likewise shows several numbers and dates. This document is the Japanese national phase of a PCT application. Three of the dates refer to the PCT application. One of these (item (86)(22)) is the PCT filing date and the other two (item (87), second occurrence) are publication dates. As in the example of a U.S. application based on a PCT application (Figure 5.2), the Japanese patent in Figure 5.10 claims its PCT filing date as the filing date in Japan. Also shown are two publication dates for the Japanese patent itself (items (24) and (45)). The effective date of this document itself is the earliest of its own publication dates (item (24)). Nevertheless, the particulars of the related PCT application in items (86)(22), (86), and (87) indicate that PCT application is also prior art and has an earlier publication, and hence effective, date. The PCT application will most likely be identical in its disclosure to the Japanese patent (although in a different language). If the Japanese patent did not have a related PCT application, the Japanese patent itself would be the only prior art document with the same disclosure, with its earliest publication date (item (24)) as its effective date.

The last document in this series is the cover page of a patent granted in the People's Republic of China (Figure 5.11), with dates and numbers analogous to those of the Japanese patent (Figure 5.10). If no PCT application were indicated, the effective date of the

(19)

Europäisches Patentamt

European Patent Office

Office européen des brevets

(11) **EP 0 739 941 A1**

(12) **EUROPEAN PATENT APPLICATION**

(43) Date of publication:
30.10.1996 Bulletin 1996/44

(51) Int. Cl.⁶: **C08L 23/16**, C08L 23/10, C08L 53/00

(21) Application number: 96106780.8

(22) Date of filing: 29.04.1996

(84) Designated Contracting States:
DE FR GB IT

(30) Priority: 28.04.1995 JP 106762/95
28.04.1995 JP 106763/95
28.04.1995 JP 106764/95
28.04.1995 JP 106765/95
28.04.1995 JP 106766/95

(71) Applicants:
• SUMITOMO CHEMICAL COMPANY LIMITED
Osaka-shi, Osaka 541 (JP)
• TOYOTA JIDOSHA KABUSHIKI KAISHA
Aichi-ken (JP)

(72) Inventors:
• Sadatoshi, Hajime
Ichihara-shi (JP)
• Suzuki, Haruyuki
Sodegaura-shi (JP)
• Miyake, Yuichi
Nagoya-shi (JP)
• Nomura, Takao
Toyota-shi (JP)
• Nishio, Takeyoshi
Okazaki-shi (JP)

(74) Representative: VOSSIUS & PARTNER
Siebertstrasse 4
81675 München (DE)

(54) **Thermoplastic resin composition**

(57) A thermoplastic resin composition with improved low-temperature impact strength and rigidity against heat, comprising (I) 10-40% by weight of a mixture of (a) 10-50% by weight of a propylene homopolymer and/or an ethylene-propylene block copolymer (an isotactic pentad fraction of a propylene homopolymer portion being 0.98 or above) and (b) 50-90% by weight of an olefin-based copolymer rubber, said mixture having been dynamically heat treated in the presence of an organic peroxide and a crosslinking agent, (II) 20-85% by weight of a propylene homopolymer and/or an ethylene-propylene block copolymer (an isotactic pentad fraction of a propylene homopolymer portion being 0.98 or above and a melt index of the propylene homopolymer portion being 30-150 g/10 min), and (III) 5-40% by weight of an inorganic filler.

EP 0 739 941 A1

Printed by Rank Xerox (UK) Business Services
2.13.8/3.4

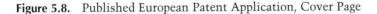

Figure 5.8. Published European Patent Application, Cover Page

⑲ 日本国特許庁 (JP)　　　　　　　⑪ 特 許 出 願 公 開

⑫ 公 開 特 許 公 報 (A)　　　昭56—136841

⑤Int. Cl.³	識別記号	庁内整理番号	⑬公開　昭和56年(1981)10月26日
C 08 L　71/04		6911—4 J	
C 08 K　3/22	C A M	6911—4 J	発明の数　1
3/26	C A M	6911—4 J	審査請求　有
C 08 L　25/00		7919—4 J	
// C 08 J　7/04		7415—4 F	（全 8 頁）

⑤改良されたメッキ特性を有する新規なポリフ
エ二レンエーテル樹脂組成物

⑳特　　　願　昭55—41631

㉒出　　　願　昭55(1980) 3 月31日

⑫発 明 者　岡本和則
　　　　　　　川崎市多摩区生田8778第 2 向山

マンション306号

⑫発 明 者　和崎博昭
　　　　　　　堺市引野町 2 丁目110— 2

⑦出 願 人　エンジニアリングプラスチック
　　　　　　　ス株式会社
　　　　　　　大阪市西区新町一丁目 1 番17号

⑭代 理 人　弁理士　安達光雄　外 1 名

(1)

明　　細　　書

1. 発明の名称　　改良されたメッキ特性を有する
　　　　　　　　　新規なポリフエ二レンエーテル
　　　　　　　　　樹脂組成物

2. 特許請求の範囲

　1. (a) ポリフエ二レンエーテル樹脂 3 0 〜 9 5
　　　重量部、

　　(b) ビニル芳香族重合体 7 0 〜 5 重量部、

　　(c) 不飽和度の低いエラストマー 1 〜 5 0 重量部、

　　(d) MgCO₃、CaCO₃、MgO の 1 種または 2 種以上
　　　1.0 〜 3 0 重量部（前記重合体(a)、(b) および
　　　(c)の合計量 1 0 0 重量部に対して）

　　よりなる改良されたメッキ特性を有する新規な
　　ポリフエ二レンエーテル樹脂組成物。

3. 発明の詳細な説明

　　本発明は、成形品に対する改良されたメッキ
　　特性（メッキ特性とは、プラスチックとメッキ
　　した金属の結合の良否の状態すなわち、メッキ
　　密着性のことを指す）を有する新規なポリフエ
　　二レンエーテル樹脂組成物に関するものである。

(2)

　　ポリフエ二レンエーテルは、比較的高い溶融
粘度および軟化点（即ち 2 7 5 ℃以上）を有す
る機械的性質、電気的特性、耐薬品性、耐熱性
などがすぐれた熱可塑性樹脂であり、しかも耐
加水分解性、寸法安定性も良いなどの性質も備
えているために、近年非常に注目されている。
しかし上述したような望ましい特性は備えるも
ののポリフエ二レンエーテルから成形された部
品にメッキを施して商業的価値あるメッキ密着
強度を得ることが困難である。更に比較的高い
溶融粘度および軟化点は、多くの用途にとって
は、不利であると考えられている。

　　ポリフエ二レンエーテルの特性は、他の重合
体類の配合により実質的に変えられることが当
技術界で知られている。例えば米国特許第
3 3 8 3 4 3 5 号明細書には、ポリフエ二レン
エーテルの成形加工性を改良し同時にポリスチ
レンの多くの特性を向上させる手段が開示され
ている。該特許発明によればポリフエ二レンエ
ーテルとポリスチレン（変性ポリスチレンを含

Figure 5.9.　Published Japanese Patent Application (*Kokai*), Cover Page

(19)日本国特許庁（ＪＰ）　　(12) **特　許　公　報**(Ｂ２)　　(11)特許番号

特許第3459633号

(P3459633)

(45)発行日　平成15年10月20日(2003.10.20)　　　　(24)登録日　平成15年8月8日(2003.8.8)

(51)Int.Cl.⁷　　　　　　識別記号　　　　　　　　　　ＦＩ

　Ｃ１２Ｍ　　1/34　　　　　　　　　　　　　Ｃ１２Ｍ　　1/34　　　　Ａ

　　　　　　　3/00　　　　　　　　　　　　　　　　　　　3/00　　　　Ｚ

　Ｇ０１Ｎ　　1/28　　　　　　　　　　　　　Ｇ０１Ｎ　　1/28　　　　Ｗ

請求項の数3（全 15 頁）

(21)出願番号　　特願2000-574218(P2000-574218)　　　(73)特許権者　591099809

　　　　　　　　　　　　　　　　　　　　　　　　　　　　バイオーラッド　ラボラトリーズ，イン

(86)(22)出願日　平成10年9月18日(1998.9.18)　　　　　　　　コーポレイティド

　　　　　　　　　　　　　　　　　　　　　　　　　　　　アメリカ合衆国，カリフォルニア

(65)公表番号　　特表2002-526064(P2002-526064A)　　　　94547，ハーキュルズ，アルフレッド

(43)公表日　　平成14年8月20日(2002.8.20)　　　　　　　　ノーベル　ドライブ　1000

(86)国際出願番号　ＰＣＴ／ＵＳ９８／１９４９１　　(72)発明者　リー，アン　エー.

(87)国際公開番号　ＷＯ００／０１７３１７　　　　　　　　アメリカ合衆国，カリフォルニア

(87)国際公開日　平成12年3月30日(2000.3.30)　　　　　　92672，サンクレメント，ナンバー　58,

　　審査請求日　平成12年6月1日(2000.6.1)　　　　　　　　カレ　デル　セロ　1100

　　　　　　　　　　　　　　　　　　　　　　　　　　(74)代理人　100077517

　　　　　　　　　　　　　　　　　　　　　　　　　　　　弁理士　石田　敬　（外4名）

　　　　　　　　　　　　　　　　　　　　　　　　　　　審査官　鈴木　恵理子

最終頁に続く

(54)【発明の名称】　培養細胞のための二軸歪システム

1

(57)【特許請求の範囲】

【請求項1】　弾性膜に付着させた生物学的細胞に二軸歪を付与するための装置であって：

膜支持体（１２）、ここでかかる膜支持体（１２）は一端において開口部を有する管状通路、突き出した軸状の縁（４４）を有する硬質リング（４２）及び前記開口部を囲む当該膜支持体内のチャンネル（４５）を有し、ここで前記チャンネル（４５）は前記突き出した軸状の縁（４４）を摩擦嵌合で受容するようなサイズとなっている；

平面状の縁において一端が終結した開放且つ中空のシリンダー（１１）、ここでかかるシリンダー（１１）は前記管状通路内に配され、前記膜支持体（１２）及び前記シリンダー（１１）が前記開口部伝いにて固定された任意のかかる膜（１４）と同一側にある；並びに

2

ねじ込接続体を介して前記膜支持体（１２）に結合され、且つ前記シリンダー（１１）に結合した作動手段（１３）；を含んで成り、

かくして前記作動手段（１３）の前記ねじ込接続体伝いでの回転は前記シリンダー（１１）を前記管状通路内で縦方向に運動させ、これにより前記平面状の縁は回転の度合いに対応して前記開口部を介して突き出て前記開口部伝いに固定された任意の前記膜（１４）と結合し、前記膜（１４）の中央部を前記平面状の縁伝いの平面形状で二軸延伸せしめる、装置。

【請求項2】　弾性膜に付着させた生物学的細胞に二軸歪を付与するための装置であって：

膜支持体（１２）、ここでかかる膜支持体（１２）は一端において開口部を有する管状通路及びかかる開口部伝いにてかかる膜を固定するための手段（１５）を有す

Figure 5.10. *Granted Japanese Patent (Kokoku), Cover Page*

[19] 中华人民共和国国家知识产权局

[51] Int. Cl⁷

H01L 21/44

H01L 21/48 H01L 21/50

H01L 21/30 H01L 21/46

[12] **发明专利申请公开说明书**

[21] 申请号 02813931.3

[43] 公开日 2004年9月1日

[11] 公开号 CN 1526162A

[22] 申请日 2002.6.19 [21] 申请号 02813931.3

[30] 优先权

[32] 2001.7.12 [33] US [31] 09/904,583

[86] 国际申请 PCT/US2002/019501 2002.6.19

[87] 国际公布 WO2003/007362 英 2003.1.23

[85] 进入国家阶段日期 2004.1.12

[71] 申请人 RJR 聚合物股份有限公司

地址 美国加利福尼亚州

[72] 发明人 R·S·布雷甘迪 T·谢弗

K·S·梅伦 R·J·罗斯

[74] 专利代理机构 上海专利商标事务所

代理人 周承泽

权利要求书2页 说明书7页

[54] 发明名称 多种材料在电子器件的气穴封装中的应用

[57] 摘要

通过分三个独立部分——基底、侧壁和盖子——包封半导体电路器件(芯片),可以将芯片装入防潮电子封装。 先将所述芯片焊接或结合到基底上,接着将侧壁连接到基底上,最后将盖子连接到侧壁上。 对于涉及导热基底和焊接高温的过程,可在焊接时的高温下将芯片固定到基底上,接着在明显低得多的温度下将侧壁安装到基底上,这样就避免了高温对侧壁可能造成的伤害。 因此,可以使用在焊接时的高温下会损坏或变形的塑料侧壁。对于通用电子封装,如果使用塑料侧壁,就可以同时使用原本不相容的盖子材料和基底材料,而且减少或消除了由于在生产、组装、测试或使用封装时的高温下发生应力开裂而出现不合格产品的机会。

ISSN1008-4274

知识产权出版社出版

Figure 5.11. Published Chinese Patent Application, Cover Page

Chinese patent would be the indicated publication date (item [43]). In this case, however, the patent indicates two possibilities for earlier effective dates due to its indication of related documents. One of these is a published PCT application, with a publication date (item [87]) that precedes the grant date of the Chinese patent. The other is a corresponding U.S. patent application, whose data is listed as item [30], including its filing date as item [32]. The prudent investigator will obtain a copy of the published version of the corresponding U.S. application, since that document will have an effective filing date that far predates the publication date of the Chinese patent and may thus be more damaging as prior art.

Published Materials Other Than Patents

Among its definitions of prior art the patent statute cites material that is "described in a printed publication in this or a foreign country." While all of the documents listed in the previous section are "printed publications," this category goes well beyond these documents to include published materials in general. These materials include articles in technical journals, handout materials distributed at symposia, printed news media, press releases, published abstracts, and materials included in product packaging or for advertising and promotion. Technical data sheets, instruction manuals, newsletters, magazine ads, and documents made available through the Internet all fall within the category, as do funding applications and dissertations at colleges and universities. The term "printed" has no special meaning and is not limited to mechanically or electronically printed matter, and "publication" of any of these items can range from mass marketing to an extremely limited distribution to an exclusive or highly specialized group, and can occur anywhere in the world. The effective date for any of these publications is the date of publication, regardless of where publication occurs. The date of publication, and hence the effective date, is interpreted to mean the date when the printed information is made available or accessible to others without the need to obtain permission from the author or publisher.

Business or Commercial Activities, Transactions, and Communications

This category includes uses in a commercial or production setting, and sales or offers for sale. A use in a commercial or production setting may occur when an invention is incorporated in a plant process or in a product delivered to, or service performed for, clients or customers with whom there is an existing or potential business relationship. The use will qualify as prior art regardless of whether knowledge of the use was made available or accessible to the public or to others in the industry, and generally regardless of the extent of the use and whether or not it was a revenue-generating use, and if so, how much revenue was generated. A sale or offer for sale will qualify as prior art regardless of the volume sold or offered, regardless of whether the sale price or offering price is the market price, and regardless of whether the buyer or offeree is a U.S. citizen or resident. The effective date of the use, sale, or offer for sale as prior art is the date that the use began or the sale or offer was made. This category is subject to a geographical limitation, however: only those uses, sales, or offers that occur within the United States will qualify.

Exceptions within this category are uses, sales, and offers whose overriding purpose is experimentation. These exceptions are widely claimed, difficult to establish, and often denied, since the determinations are matters of judgment arrived at after consideration of all available evidence. The experimentation must be related to functionality or technical viability rather than economic concerns, and individual factors that are persuasive in some cases may be deemed insufficient in others.

Oral Disclosures

This category rarely arises since its existence and content are difficult to establish. Nevertheless, oral disclosures anywhere in the world by themselves, i.e., aside from published printed matter, can qualify as prior art provided that the disclosures are not made under confidential circumstances. Typical examples include presentations at symposia and conferences and presentations to potential investors.

OVERCOMING THE EFFECTIVE DATE: CANCELING PRIOR ART STATUS BY SHOWING AN EARLIER ACT OF INVENTION

A feature of the U.S. patent law that is distinct from the patent laws of most other jurisdictions in the identification of prior art is a recognition of the date on which an invention was invented. U.S. law allows an inventor to remove a reference (or any prior art activity) from consideration as prior art by presenting evidence that the invention was actually invented before the effective date of the reference. This presentation of evidence is commonly termed "swearing back" of a reference. The evidence that the inventor cites in swearing back of the reference can be as rudimentary as the inventor's mental conception of the invention or as advanced as a reduction to practice by constructing a prototype, preparing a sample, or successfully performing a test run. To successfully swear back, the evidence must be reasonably commensurate in scope with the invention as it is claimed in the patent application, and it must be documented in a form that contains enough description or information to indicate that the concept had in fact been formed or the prototype or sample actually made or the test actually performed. The evidence can be as simple as handwritten notes or as detailed as a research report. Corroboration of the evidence by a witness is not strictly required but can add to the persuasiveness of the evidence and lessen its vulnerability to challenge. A statement of the actual date on which the evidence was created is likewise not required, nor even of the date on which the act occurred. It is instead sufficient to state that one or both precede the effective date that the evidence seeks to predate. If much time has passed between the date indicated by the evidence and the inventor's filing date, however, it may be necessary to explain the reason for the delay to show that despite the delay the inventor was diligent in applying for the patent and had neither abandoned nor purposely suppressed the invention. Until any "swearing back" is done, the filing date of the inventor's patent application serves as the demarcation date separating references or activities that qualify as prior art from those that do not.

Inventors do not however have an unlimited freedom to swear back of all prior art. By an explicit provision in the patent statute, prior art in the form of published matter or commercial activity (i.e., a use for a commercial purpose, a sale or an offer for sale) cannot be sworn back of if more than one year has passed between the publication date or the use, sale, or offer date and the inventor's filing date. The identification of prior art in general, therefore, is a two-level inquiry: first, whether the law will permit the inventor to "swear back" of the presumed prior art, and second, where swearing back is permissible, whether an act of invention occurred early enough to permit the inventor to use that act to swear

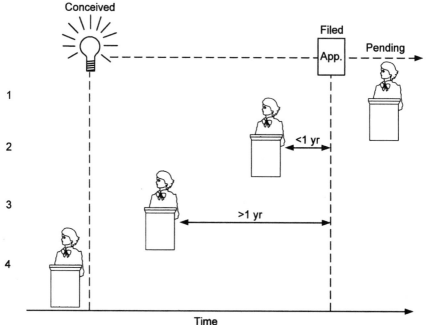

Figure 5.12. Time Scale: Oral Presentations as Prior Art

back and whether that act is adequately supported by documentary evidence.

Figures 5.12, 5.13, and 5.14 each depict a series of scenarios that illustrate swearing back and its limitations. The scenarios shown in Figure 5.12 represent prior art that includes neither publication, patenting, nor commercial use (including sales or offers for sale), and therefore presents no bar to swearing back. Prior art that meets this description, and is represented in Figure 5.12 by a speaker at a podium, includes oral presentations without the distribution of printed materials, or with only those printed materials that do not contain sufficient disclosure to enable the reader to practice or implement the information conveyed in the oral presentation. This prior art is the least likely to be encountered, but is included here for comparison with other prior art categories shown in the succeeding figures. In the scenarios of Figure 5.13, the prior art, which is represented by the open book symbol, is either a publication or a commercial use, and therefore imposes the one-year limitation on the ability to be removed by swearing back. The prior art in

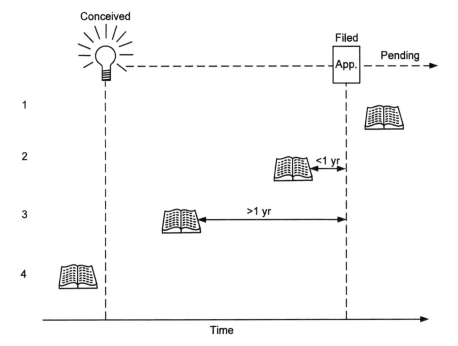

Figure 5.13. Time Scale: Published Materials as Prior Art

Figure 5.13 are activities whose actual dates are the same as their effective dates. This constitutes all forms of prior art other than U.S. patents and patent-related documents, and includes patents and patent applications published by any non-U.S. patent authority (including the PCT and various geographical regions and countries throughout the world), published material other than patents, commercial uses, sales, and offers for sale. The scenarios of Figure 5.14 involve prior art in the form of U.S. patents and patent-related documents, including pre-grant publications, defensive publications, and statutory invention registrations, which likewise impose the one-year limitation on swearing back. For each of these documents, the effective date of the document as prior art, represented by the "Application" symbol, differs from the date of the document itself, represented by the "Patent" symbol.

Each of the three figures is a series of one-dimensional time lines in which time progresses from left to right. The line at the top of each figure represents the inventor and shows two main events in the sequence of applying for a U.S. patent: the date of conception of the invention as represented by the light bulb symbol, and the date of

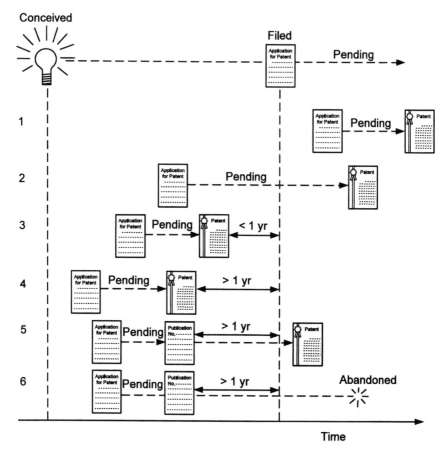

Figure 5.14. Time Scale: Patents as Prior Art

filing the patent application in the United States as represented by
the labeled rectangle. (The filing date is the date recognized as such
by the USPTO, and may be either the date on which the application
was sent directly to the USPTO or a date that the application was
sent to a patent authority of another jurisdiction and was afforded the
status of a U.S. filing date in accordance with the terms of an international patent treaty. Treaties of this kind are discussed elsewhere
in this book.) The time represented by the dashed line between the
conception date and the filing date may be occupied by events such as
prototype construction or sample preparation, testing, consultations
with a patent attorney, the preparation of the patent application, and
reviews by the inventor of various drafts of the application before the
application is ready for filing. The dashed line to the right of the filing

date represents the period during which the patent application is pending. (The date of issuance of the patent is not shown, since it is not relevant to this discussion.) The lines below the top line of each figure represent individual pieces of presumed prior art, each having different dates. Each form of prior art is represented by a symbol whose horizontal position relative to the symbols in the top line indicates the relative timing of each occurrence.

In Figure 5.12, four oral presentations are shown, ranging in time from before the inventor's conception of the invention (Presentation No. 4) to after the filing date of the patent application (Presentation No. 1). An oral presentation made after the filing date (Presentation No. 1) will not be raised as prior art since the effective date of the presentation (its only date, in fact) is antedated by the inventor's filing date. An oral presentation made before the inventor's conception date (Presentation No. 1) presents no opportunity for swearing back since the inventor's conception did not occur early enough. Presentation Nos. 2 and 3 both present possibilities for swearing back since they each occur subsequent to the inventor's conception date. The fact that Presentation No. 2 occurred less than one year before the filing date and Presentation No. 3 more than one year before the filing date is not relevant, since the statute presents no bar to swearing back of this type of prior art.

In Figure 5.13, a book symbol represents prior art in the form of non-U.S.-patent published materials, including foreign patents and patent applications, and commercial uses, including sales and offers for sale. For published materials, the position of book symbol along the time line represents the date of publication, and for commercial uses, the position represents date of the first occurrence of the use.

The simplest scenarios shown are Nos. 1 and 4. The timing of the publication or use in Scenario No. 1 (as represented by the position of the symbol) is after the filing date of the inventor's patent application, and is therefore never considered as prior art. The publication or use in Scenario No. 4 predates the filing date and is thus prior art until sworn back of. The inventor is however unable to swear back of the publication or use since the inventor has no evidence to swear to, i.e., no conception of the invention or any activity relating to the invention occurs prior to the date of the publication. In both Scenario Nos. 2 and 3, the publication or use occurs between the inventor's conception date and the filing date of the patent application, and in both cases is deemed prior art relative to the invention until the inventor removes the prior art status by swearing back. In Scenario No. 2, swearing back is permissible since the time period between the publication date and the inventor's filing date is less than one year, and the fact that conception occurred well before the publication date indicates that swearing back can indeed be done, provided that supporting documentation exists. In Scenario No. 3, the inventor's conception likewise predates the publication or use, but this is of no value in overcoming the publication, since more than one year has passed between the publication or use date and the filing date, thereby barring the inventor from swearing back.

A more complex set of scenarios is represented by Figure 5.14, where the presumed prior art is a U.S. patent-related document, i.e., either a patent, a pre-grant publication, a defensive publication, or a statutory invention registration. As mentioned above, the date of each document (i.e., the issue date of a patent and the publication date of a pre-grant publication, defensive publication, or statutory invention registration) in these scenarios differs from the effective date of the document. Each scenario therefore includes at least two symbols, one (labeled "Application for Patent") representing the filing date and the other (labeled "Patent") the date of the document. One scenario includes both a pre-grant publication and an issued patent, for a total of three symbols. In all, six scenarios are represented, with time again progressing from left to right, while the line at the top of the figure represents the inventor and shows the date of conception of the invention and the filing date of the patent application in the United States, using the same symbols as the preceding figures. All cases, however, list a single filing date for simplification, although it is understood that when any document represented in this figure claims a benefit from one or more related applications, the effective date is the filing date of the earliest of these related applications.

Document No. 1 is not considered as prior art since its effective date (i.e., its filing date) occurs subsequent to the filing date of the patent application represented by the line at the top of the chart. Document Nos. 2 through 6 all present at least an initial status as prior art, since each has an effective date that predates the filing date of the application at the top of the chart. In each case as well, the effective date falls subsequent to the conception date shown in the top line, presenting the inventor in the top line with the possibility of using the conception date to swear back of each document provided that the inventor is not barred from doing so by the one-year limitation. Document No. 2 is a patent that was not published prior to issuance, and since its issue date occurs subsequent to the filing date of the application under consideration, the inventor is at liberty to swear back and remove this document from consideration as prior art. Document No. 3 is likewise a patent that was not published prior to issuance. The issue date of Document No. 3 does fall before the filing date of the application under consideration, but the period between the issue date of the document and the filing date of the application at the top of the chart is less than one year. The inventor is thus at liberty here as well to swear back of this document with the inventor's conception date and remove the prior art status of the document. This capability is not present in the case of Document No. 4, another patent issuing without a prior publication, since the patent issue date is more than one year prior to the filing date of the application under consideration. The symbols shown in the line representing Document No. 5 include both a pre-grant publication of an application and the patent issuing on the application. While the patent postdates the filing date in the top line, the pre-grant publication occurs before the filing date by more than one year. Thus, because of the pre-grant publication, the inventor is barred from swearing back of either the pre-grant publication or the patent. Document No. 6 is a pre-grant publication of an application that is abandoned before maturing into a patent, and is included to demonstrate that the subsequent abandonment of the application does not remove its status as prior art once it has been published. If the time gap between publication and the filing date of the application under consideration is greater than one year, as shown, the inventor is barred from swearing back of the document.

Worthy of note in Figure 5.14 is the fact that a patent or pre-grant publication that is issued or published after the filing date of the application against which it is cited is still prior art until sworn back of, and if the evidence available for swearing back is incomplete or not sufficiently early, the reference cannot be overcome. Thus, a patent or pre-grant publication that entirely deprives an individual's invention of novelty may not emerge until well after the individual has prepared and filed a patent application. The individual may thus have no way of knowing that the expenditures made in preparing and filing the application were fruitless until after they were made. The chances of this occurring are reduced however by the publication of patent applications at a fixed period of time (eighteen months) after filing.

BEYOND PRIOR ART: THE QUESTION
OF CONFLICTING PATENTS

When a patent or published patent application arises as prior art, one is always tempted to look at the claims of the document to see what the party who filed the document is seeking to patent. Recall that earlier in this chapter we stated that the claims of a patent or published application are generally of no significance as prior art. Specifically, one cannot dismiss a patent-related document as prior art simply because the claims of the document do not recite the distinctive features of one's own invention, since despite their absence from the claims, those features may be disclosed at some other location in the same document. When the claims of the document do recite the distinctive features as one's own invention, however, the claims of the document are indeed significant and the document assumes an importance beyond its status as prior art: it raises the possibility of a dispute to decide which of the two competing parties should be awarded a patent on that invention. The party that is not awarded the patent loses not only its power to exclude others from practicing the invention, but also its ability to use the invention itself. Patents or patent applications with conflicting claims thus present a potential obstacle to one's freedom to operate as well as an obstacle to patentability.

When different inventors compete for a patent on the same invention, the patent is awarded to the inventor who is the first to have invented the invention. This first-to-invent approach distinguishes U.S. patent law from the patent laws of other jurisdictions where competing claims are awarded on a first-to-file basis, i.e., to the party that is the first to submit its patent application. The determination of which party is the first to invent occurs in an often extensive legal proceeding known as an "interference." Interferences are the subject of another chapter of this book, but certain points bear relevance to this discussion of prior art.

First, interferences can be declared between issued patents, between pending patent applications (published or not), between a patent and a pending application, or between either a patent or an application and a statutory invention registration, and any number of competing parties can be involved. Second, an interference can be declared even if only a single claim from one document recites the same invention as a single claim in the competing document, regardless of any other claims in either of the two documents. The competing claims must however recite the same invention, using wording that is either identical or equivalent. Thus, the limitations defining the scope of the claim of one document must be the same limitations that define the scope of the claim of the other document, i.e., the claims must be coextensive in scope. Documents with claims that merely overlap do not qualify for an interference, nor do those in which the claims of one are broader than and dominate (fully encompass) the claims of the other.

Third, one of the features of prior art treatment applies to interferences as well: the one-year publication bar. Thus, where one of the documents in which the competing claims reside has been published before the filing date of the other document and more than one year has passed between the publication date of the first document and the filing date of the second, no interference will be declared, and the claim will be awarded to the party with the earlier publication (and hence the earlier filing date).

When a single patent or published application functions both as a prior art document and as a document for a potential interference, the resolution of one of these two issues may not also resolve the other. When one party to an interference prevails by establishing an earlier date of invention, this will indeed amount to a "swearing back" of the filing date of the competing document as well, since the filing date will necessarily be later in time. Interferences can be terminated, however, for reasons other than a determination of the first to invent and for reasons that do not affect the status of any particular document as prior art relative to the other. Likewise, the prior art status of a patent or application can be removed by swearing back of the filing date of the document, without addressing the invention date of the invention reflected in the document. Thus, prior art issues and interference issues must be considered independently.

Chapter 6

Novelty and Nonobviousness: The Second Step in Determining Patentability

Once the prior art is identified, an invention can be evaluated for novelty and nonobviousness. While these are only two of the three fundamental criteria for patentability (the third is utility), these two alone are determined relative to the prior art. Novelty and nonobviousness are not independent criteria, but rather a sequential analysis, with novelty as the threshold inquiry and nonobviousness reached only when novelty has been established. If novelty is not present, arguments and demonstrations to show nonobviousness will not overcome the prior art and will not be entertained, either by the USPTO or patent authorities in general, or by a court of law. By understanding where and how novelty can be found, and how particular types of novelty set their own standards for determinations of nonobviousness, one can properly evaluate patentability and frame an invention by selecting its boundaries or parameters in a manner that will allow both criteria to be met.

NOVELTY

Novelty is satisfied by identifying a difference between the invention and the prior art without assessing the quality of the difference. Differences that meet this standard can assume any of a variety of forms. The simplest differences are those that place the invention entirely outside the scope of the prior art. This can be done by placing the boundaries of the invention at locations where the invention neither overlaps nor shares a boundary with the prior art. For certain inventions, novelty can also be found even if the invention and the prior art overlap. The result in these cases is often the opposite of what simple logic might suggest: novelty is generally not found in inventions that expand the prior art while still encompassing it, and yet novelty can be found in inventions that fall entirely within the scope of the prior art if the inventions are more narrowly defined with boundaries not disclosed in the prior art. In still further inventions, novelty can be found in the manner in which an invention is expressed, i.e., as a new use of a known material or device; as a new combination of components previously known only by themselves or in other combinations; or as a composition, component, or process used or performed in a new environment.

Novelty without Overlap

Principal methods of casting an invention to avoid overlap with the prior art are (1) substitution, (2) change of a parameter, and (3) elimination of a component.

In a claim to a combination, a substitution can occur by replacing a component of the combination with a different component. In a claim to a process, substitution can occur by changing a material used in the process or changing a material that the process is operated on.

Example 1—A combination-type composition of matter
meeting novelty by the substitution of a component of
the composition

Prior art: A cosmetic product on the market, consisting of an all-purpose hand, face, and body lotion containing stearic acid, lanolin, mineral oil, cetyl alcohol, triethanolamine, methyl and propyl parabens, and water

Invention: A lotion containing all of the components of the prior art cosmetic product except mineral oil, and substituting castor oil for the mineral oil

Example 2—A process meeting novelty by the
substitution of a material used in the process

Prior art: A review article in a semiconductor industry trade journal describing ion implantation processes for doping semiconductor substrates, listing ten examples of doping elements

Invention: An ion implantation process identical to one of the processes cited in the review article except for the use of a doping element not among those listed in the article

The changing of a parameter can likewise occur in both composition claims and process claims. An example of a composition parameter is the proportions of the components. Examples of parameters in a process are the temperature range, the concentration range, the sequence of process steps, and the proportion of starting materials.

Example 3—A combination-type composition of matter meeting novelty by changing the relative amounts of the composition components

Prior art: A topical skin care product containing vitamin D, vitamin E, and lecithin in combination as active ingredients, with vitamins D and E as major components while lecithin constitutes only 0.1% by weight of the product

Invention: A topical skin care product containing vitamin D, vitamin E, and lecithin in combination as active ingredients, with the lecithin constituting 3–7% of the product

Example 4—A process meeting novelty by changing the values of process parameters

Prior art: A patent describing the use of ultrasound in a process for devulcanizing scrap rubber and recommending a 20–30 kHz range of ultrasound frequency and a minimum time of 30 seconds for ultrasound exposure

Invention: A process involving the use of ultrasound for devulcanizing scrap rubber but at an ultrasound frequency of 35–60 kHz and for a period of 2–5 seconds

The elimination of an element or a component renders a combination or process novel when the prior art discloses the combination only in full or the process only as a complete sequence of steps.

Example 5—A combination-type composition of matter meeting novelty by eliminating a component of the combination

Prior art: Topical creams on the market that include preservatives, one such preservative being commonly used in combination

with a buffering agent to maintain the effectiveness of the preservative

Invention: A topical cream containing the particular preservative
without the buffering agent

Example 6—A process meeting novelty
by eliminating a process step

Prior art: A published patent application describing a gas-phase
chemical reaction performed over a solid catalyst in a flow-
through reactor, including a preheating stage for the reactants and
a rapid cooling stage to quench the product mixture immediately
upon the emergence of the mixture from the reactor

Invention: The same reaction being performed over the same
solid catalyst in the same flow-through reactor with the same
quenching step but without the preheating stage

Novelty with Overlap

Inventions that fall entirely or partially within the scope of a
disclosure in the prior art and still meet the novelty requirement
tend to occur as a subgenus (or one or more species) of a prior art
genus.

A species is a single, specifically characterized element. In
composition-of-matter-type inventions, a species commonly encountered in patents is a combination of components, each component
specified both in terms of its identity and its amount relative to the
other components. In process-type inventions, a species can be a
processing step of which all processing parameters are specified.
These parameters may include a specific temperature, pressure,
exposure time, and composition of the atmosphere in which the
step is performed, and any other process details that the process
operator will need to follow in order to perform the step according to
exact specifications.

A genus is a class of species all sharing a common feature or all
recognized as being a member of the class, particularly where the
class has a recognized name. Examples of genera are inert gases,
noble metals, soft magnetic alloys, and p-type doping elements.
Genera are also established by expressing a particular feature as a
range or by leaving one or more features unspecified. A generic

expression of a chemical reaction may thus be one that omits one or more operating conditions such as the temperature, the residence time, or the proportions or concentrations of the reactants, or one that recites a temperature range ("800–1,500°C," for example) rather than a specific temperature, or a pressure range ("superatmospheric," for example) rather than a specific pressure.

A subgenus is a range or class falling within a genus but not including the entire genus. The range of 50–70°C is thus a subgenus of 10–100°C; a reaction mixture with reactants in proportions defined as stoichiometric to 20% excess of one reactant is a subgenus of the reaction mixture without specified proportions. The number of species encompassed by a subgenus or genus can be known ("inert gases," "noble metals") or capable of precise determination, although in most cases the number is indeterminable and a particular species' inclusion is known only by its conformance with the boundaries of the genus ("a film having a thickness of 10–100 microns," "a polymer having a dielectric constant of 2.5–10").

The genus-species or genus-subgenus relationship is also present in combinations versus subcombinations or components. A class of compositions in which each composition contains at a minimum components A and B, for example, fully encompasses and exceeds in size a class in which each composition contains at a minimum components A, B, and C. Since neither class *excludes* compositions that contain components in addition to those specified, the A-B class is generic to the A-B-C class. Similarly, a disclosure of a particular property of species D that makes the species suitable for a particular use can be generic to the use of species D in combination with species E for the same use, if the original species D disclosure does not require that D be used alone. (If the original disclosure does state that species D is effective only if used alone, the situation is not a genus-species relationship but rather one without overlap and thus within the scope of the "Novelty Without Overlap" section above.)

Example 1—A combination-type composition of matter meeting novelty by claiming substances in combination that were previously known only individually

Prior art: A technical paper on antioxidants reporting the results of a study of the antioxidant properties of individual vitamins, listing vitamins A, C, and E

Invention: A dietary supplement for antioxidant effect combining vitamins A, C, and E in a single dosage form

Example 2—A combination-type composition of matter
meeting novelty by claiming a combination of components
one of which was previously known for the same use

Prior art: A technical paper on the antioxidant properties of vitamin A and the effectiveness of this vitamin as an active ingredient in a skin care product by virtue of its antioxidant activity, with only a general reference to possible additional components of the product

Invention: A topical skin lotion combining vitamin A with lecithin

Example 3—A process meeting novelty by combining
steps previously known individually for the same purpose

Prior art: A European patent disclosing a process involving the application of epitaxial layers by chemical vapor deposition; and a Japanese patent disclosing the application of epitaxial layers by a sputtering technique

Invention: A process in which epitaxial layers are applied by a sequence of steps beginning with chemical vapor deposition and concluding with sputtering

Example 4—A subgenus meeting novelty relative
to a genus

Prior art: A published patent application on supersonic rockets disclosing metal oxides as a class of materials from which the nose cones are made, and mentioning alumina as an example with no specific mention of other examples

Invention: A rocket nose cone formed from titania, yttria, or a combination of metal oxides that includes either titania, yttria, or both

Example 5—Subgenera meeting novelty relative to genera

Prior art: An oral presentation at a steel industry symposium with handout materials, describing a process for forming a carbon steel alloy with a carbon content of up to 3.0% by first heating the alloy components to full austenitization followed by cooling to convert part of the austenite to martensite, while allowing wide latitude in the cooling rate by stating it as a range of 500–2,000 deg C/min

Invention: A process for forming a carbon steel by limiting the carbon content to a maximum of 0.35% and limiting the cooling rate to the range of 800–1,200 deg C/min

The reverse of the genus-species or genus-subgenus relationship, i.e., inventing a genus that encompasses a prior art species or subgenus, will not satisfy novelty, even if the recognition and identification of the genus are themselves a true discovery. Recognition of this type often arises when one discovers a key property of an existing prior art species (material or process step, for example) that is responsible for the effectiveness or success of the species (the "Aha!" or "Now I understand why it works!" situation) but was not recognized in the prior art, and one then attempts to claim the species in terms of this key property without changing the species. The same result occurs when one expands the species to a class in which all members possess the key property. If the class is defined in a manner that does not exclude the prior art species, the class lacks novelty. If the class is defined to exclude the prior art, the class is indeed novel since the class and the prior art do not overlap.

Example 6—Lack of novelty: claiming
a genus that expands on the prior art

Prior art: An electronics trade journal article referring to an ion implantation process for doping semiconductor substrates, using chromium as the doping element

Discovery that similar species are likewise effective: The same ion implantation process but specifying the doping element as any element having an atomic mass of between 50 and 55 (an inherent feature of the prior art since the atomic mass of chromium is 52)

Example 7—Lack of novelty: claiming a genus
expressed as a key but previously unrecognized
characteristic of the prior art

Prior art: A hand, face, and body lotion on the market, containing stearic acid, lanolin, mineral oil, cetyl alcohol, triethanolamine, methyl and propyl parabens, and water

Discovery of the characteristic responsible for the effectiveness of a component: A lotion with the same composition as that of the lotion on the market but citing instead of the mineral oil an oil having a hydrophile-lipophile balance (HLB) within the range of 10–12 (an inherent feature of the prior art since the HLB of mineral oil is 10)

Example 8—Novelty present in a genus expressed as a key but previously unrecognized characteristic of the prior art, and expressly excluding the prior art

Prior art: The effectiveness of nicotine and anabasine as insecticides being known for over 200 years

Discovery of the characteristic responsible for the effectiveness of a component and claiming a class having that characteristic but expressly excluding the component: An insecticidal spray containing as an active ingredient a member of the class of compounds that bind to the acetylcholine receptor in the insect central nervous system, while explicitly excluding nicotine and anabasine from the class

Novelty by Type of Invention

Chapter 2 demonstrates that the many different types of inventions that can qualify for patent protection are limited only by one's awareness of the extent of the possibilities. The categories of invention that are most commonly recognized are (1) articles, machines, or compositions of matter, (2) methods of use, and (3) methods of manufacture. The creative inventor however can imagine any number of possibilities within each of these categories, such as improvements; systems (collections of components that are used in a coordinated manner but not necessarily joined by physical connections); data generation, processing, detection, and interpretation; methods of control, correlation, inhibition, and prevention; combinations and subcombinations; and the like. The typical innovation can indeed be claimed in different ways, often bridging the different categories, and the typical patent application does so by its inclusion of a separate independent claim for each approach to the invention. This, coupled with the understanding that novelty can exist despite an overlap with the prior art, demonstrates how one can meet the novelty requirement by selecting the manner in which the invention is expressed.

Example 1—Novelty established by expressing
the invention as a new use of a known substance

Prior art: A particular chemical compound has been described in the literature as a chelating agent useful as a carrier for metal ions to enhance contrast in magnetic resonance imaging procedures.

Invention: A method of preventing body odor by applying the same compound to the surface of the skin where it attaches to metal ions secreted by the body and thereby prevents the metal ions from performing their biological function or promoting the growth of microbes including the microbes that cause body odor

Example 2—Novelty established by a known material
used as a new material of construction of a known part

Prior art: Titanium-clad steel being widely used as a material of construction for vessels containing corrosive liquids such as aqueous chloride solutions, caustic solutions, and liquids or gases containing sulfides

Invention: An ultrasonic horn made of titanium-clad steel

Example 3—Novelty established by a known
component in a new environment

Prior art: Ultrasonics and ultrasonic horns having been widely used in ultrasonic soldering and tinning, in filtration, in forming and machining, in metal cutting, in drying applications, and in medical applications

Invention: A flow-through reactor in a petroleum processing plant, with an ultrasonic horn protruding into the reactor interior

Example 4—Novelty established by a known
component in a new environment

Prior art: A particular chlorinated phenol being used in a variety of liquid solutions used as wood preservatives for protecting wood against such pests as termites, beetles, and carpenter ants

Invention: An insect bait trap with the chlorinated phenol inside the trap

The approaches to novelty set forth in this chapter are not mutually exclusive. Combination-type inventions, for example, are cited above as examples of inventions that possess novelty by combining elements that were not previously combined, but a combination is also a new environment for individual elements of the combination. Thus, the cosmetic product of Example 1 can be expressed as a new environment for the castor oil. Inventions with new-environment novelty often can also be expressed as a new combination. Thus, the ultrasonic horn of Example 3 can be expressed as a combination with other operating units in a reaction system even though the horn and the other units operate independently. Likewise, if the insect bait trap of Example 4 contains an insect sex attractant to lure insects into the trap in addition to the chlorinated phenol, the combination of the sex attractant and chlorinated phenol can be claimed as a novel combination-type invention, even though the two components operate independently and neither one affects the activity of the other. Characterizing the novelty of an invention as a particular type may be a matter of arbitrary choice in some cases, but in others the different types offer different options for enforcement strategies. In any case, an awareness of the different approaches to novelty tends to stimulate the imagination in identifying inventions for patenting, and the inclusion of multiple approaches will generally strengthen a patent.

NONOBVIOUSNESS

Once the invention is deemed to possess novelty by virtue of a difference between it and the prior art, the nonobviousness requirement looks to the quality of the difference. The nonobviousness requirement is expressed in the patent statute as follows:

> "A patent may not be obtained ... if the differences between the subject matter sought to be patented and the prior art are such that the subject matter as a whole would have been obvious at the time the invention was made to a person having ordinary skill in the art to which said subject matter pertains."

One is often tempted to believe that "ordinary skill in the art" is a distinct level of expertise, but in truth the manner in which "ordinary skill" is characterized depends on whether one is attempting to support the patentability of an invention or to show the invention to be unpatentable. The "person having ordinary skill in the art" is thus a legal fiction, and in practice, the phrase is more of a conclusion rather than a standard by which the conclusion can be reached. Nonobviousness is best defined as a determination of whether the difference that constitutes novelty is legally deemed sufficient to support the grant of a patent. In many cases, in fact, the presence or absence of nonobviousness is largely a question of how vigorously an invention is argued and the extent of any extraneous evidence that is supplied to support the argument.

From a practical standpoint, however, certain arguments or showings are generally successful in establishing nonobviousness. The appropriate argument or showing varies with the nature of the invention and the prior art and tends to fall within one of three groups of invention–versus–prior art situations. The first group are those in which the difference between the invention and the prior art is great enough that the invention is inherently nonobvious. Typical inventions of this group are those in which the ability of the invention to function at all is beyond any reasonable expectation from the prior art. The second group are those in which the ability of the invention to function for its intended purpose is contrary to a clear prediction or statement in the prior art. For inventions of this type, the prior art is said to "teach away" from the invention by containing an explicit or implicit statement that the invention will not function. The third group are those in which the prior art, while not disclosing the invention, nevertheless suggests, or creates the logical expectation, that the invention will indeed function, but not as well as it actually does. Inventions of this group provide a benefit beyond anything suggested by the prior art, the benefit typically occurring as an unusual or unexpected improvement either in a characteristic that is acknowledged by the prior art or a complementary characteristic.

As in the novelty discussions above, nonobviousness within these groups is best understood by examples.

Inherent Nonobviousness

One type of invention that is inherently nonobvious is the replacement of a material or component with another that is not known to be an equivalent and yet is shown to serve an equivalent function. The inherent nonobviousness arises from a lack of knowledge that the original and the replacement have common characteristics, especially those characteristics that are useful in the context of the invention. Inherent nonobviousness can also arise from a change of a parameter or operating condition to such a degree that the change is beyond any logical extension of the original and yet is not detrimental to the ability of the invention to function or to the final result.

Example 1—Nonobviousness by the substitution of a material of different character

Prior art: Products requiring cold storage are housed in enclosures whose walls are constructed from hollow panels that are filled with insulating materials such as vermiculite, expanded perlite, and foamed plastic.

Invention: A cold storage enclosure whose wall panels contain aluminum mesh as a filler in place of the fillers of the prior art, the aluminum mesh providing equivalent thermal insulation

Example 2—Nonobviousness by a large change in an operating parameter

Prior art: A published patent application describing a gas-phase chemical reaction performed over a solid catalyst in a flow-through reactor in which the reactor temperature is controlled by a coolant jacket to maintain the gases at a temperature below 200°C

Invention: The same reaction is performed in the same reactor but at a temperature within the range of 300–450°C with essentially no loss in product purity.

Inherent nonobviousness can also reside in the elimination of a component or process step as in the first section above, provided that the function of the component or process step is not lost by its elimination.

Example 3—Nonobviousness by the elimination of a component in a combination without loss of the function of the component

Prior art: Topical creams that include preservatives to keep the active ingredient viable over a long shelf life, one such preservative being used in combination with a buffering agent to optimize the effectiveness of the preservative

Invention: A topical cream that contains the same preservative but without a buffering agent and yet with no reduction in the long-term viability of the active ingredient

Example 4—Nonobviousness by the elimination of a process step without loss of product quality

Prior art: A published patent application describing a gas-phase chemical reaction performed over a solid catalyst in a flow-through reactor, including a preheating stage for the reactants in order to achieve a high product yield and product purity

Invention: The inventors discovering that with a seemingly minor change in the physical form of the solid catalyst, the preheating stage can be eliminated entirely with no loss in yield or purity

Nonobviousness over Prior Art That "Teaches Away"

An inventor claiming to have performed a successful experiment that is identical to an experiment reported in the literature, but with negative results, may have a difficult time convincing the patent authorities that the inventor's results were accurate, reliable, or persuasive. Nevertheless, if an invention truly functions in a manner contrary to the conventional wisdom or general knowledge, the invention is indeed an advance in the state of the art and worthy of patent protection. Invention–versus–prior art situations in which this typically arises are those in which the prior art contains a general statement that something cannot be done while the invention lies in the discovery that the generalization is overbroad, or in the discovery of a way to achieve what was thought to be unachievable.

Example 1—Nonobviousness in the discovery that a generalization is overbroad

Prior art: A series of papers published in technical journals describing a certain class of chemical compounds each containing a common chiral center causing the compound to exist as a pair of optical isomers, the literature stating that of various methods of synthesizing compounds within the class, the result is always a racemic mixture (equal amounts of the two optical isomers), even though the activity that the compounds are useful for is attributable to only one of the isomers

Invention: Discovering that for a subset of the generic class that is not specifically defined in the literature, one of the synthesis methods actually does produce the one desirable isomer to the exclusion of the other

Example 2—Nonobviousness in the discovery of a way to achieve what the prior art states is unachievable

Prior art: Conventional knowledge in the metallurgical industry is that a titanium alloy with an α-phase crystal structure can be annealed without transformation of the crystal structure to the β-phase if the annealing temperature is limited to 500°C or below.

Invention: The discovery that by including an additional alloying element in the titanium alloy, annealment without transformation to the β-phase can be achieved at temperatures above 500°C

Nonobviousness by the Showing of Unexpectedly Beneficial Results

Differences that are not large enough or otherwise not of a character to be inherently nonobvious are *prima facie* obvious, i.e., obvious until shown otherwise. The prior art in these cases thus creates a presumption of obviousness that is open to rebuttal by the presentation of evidence, commonly in the form of test results. Where for example the prior art suggests equivalence among a group of alternatives, test data showing any improvement at all may overcome the presumption. Likewise, where the prior art suggests an additive result by use of a combination, the presumption can be overcome by test data showing a synergistic result.

Example 1—A nonobvious subset of a prior art set

Prior art: A patent disclosing sodalime glass and listing silica, sodium oxide, and calcium oxide as typical components of the glass, with broad concentration ranges for each

Invention: Sodalime glass with the sodium oxide content confined to a narrow range, supported by test data comparing glasses whose sodium oxide is within the narrow range with those out-side the narrow range and showing that those within the narrow range have a markedly higher spectral transmission

Example 2—Another example of a nonobvious
subset of a prior art set

Prior art: A treatise on topical formulations consisting of porous microscopic particles with active liquid agents inside the pores of the particles, the treatise showing that the pore size distribution of the particles is a bell curve with a single maximum

Invention: A topical formulation consisting of particles with particle sizes and active liquid agents included among those listed in the treatise, but with a bimodal pore size distribution in the form of two bell curves rather than the single, larger bell curve of the treatise, supported by experimental data showing that particles whose pore size distribution is bimodal release the active agent in a more continuous manner than particles whose pore size distribution is a single bell curve

Example 3—A nonobvious combination demonstrating
synergism relative to its components

Prior art: Literature from a supplier to the semiconductor in-dustry listing a selection of chemical products suitable for use in forming a mask over an SiO_2 substrate for a patterned etching step in a process for the application of microcircuitry to the substrate

Invention: The discovery that two of the products when used in combination produces a mask that is more stable upon exposure to high-energy etching than either of the two materials used indi-vidually

Example 4—A combination possessing
nonobvious qualities

Prior art: A published European patent application disclosing cardiovascular stents made of a nickel-aluminum alloy, and a U.S. patent disclosing cardiovascular stents made of a nickel-titanium alloy, both alloys having a shape memory permitting them to be distorted at temperatures below body temperature to facilitate their insertion and then to spontaneously resume their shape when brought to body temperature

Invention: The discovery that a stent formed from a new alloy that combines nickel with both aluminum and titanium as alloying elements resumes its shape more completely and in less time than stents of either the nickel-aluminum alloy or the nickel-titanium alloy

Improvements that are not unexpected will not rebut the presumption of obviousness. Typical among these improvements are those occurring in a novel setting but through a known mechanism.

Example 5—Obviousness not overcome: expected result
from a known modification in a novel environment

Prior art: A published paper by a university researcher reporting a liquid-phase chemical reaction performed in the laboratory at moderate temperature

Expected effect from a known modification: The same reaction performed at a temperature 10 degrees higher to increase the reaction rate

Example 6—Obviousness not overcome: introduction of
a component to serve a function the component is
known to serve in an analogous environment

Prior art: General knowledge in the rubber industry that butyl rubber can be crosslinked by a peroxide crosslinking agent and that ethylene glycol dimethacrylate is useful as an additive for increasing peroxide crosslinking efficiency in rubbers in general although not previously used for butyl rubber

Expected activity of a known additive: The use of ethylene glycol dimethacrylate to increase the peroxide crosslinking efficiency of butyl rubber

CONCLUSION

The scenarios presented in this chapter are not intended to be comprehensive. The nature of the invention itself and the state of the art in any given technology will set their own parameters for novelty and nonobviousness, and as has been shown, the range and variety of inventions that are susceptible to patent protection are large and possibly limitless. This suggests that new and imaginative ways of meeting these requirements will continue to emerge. The starting point however for patenting in any technology will be any innovation that provides a benefit, any problem or shortcoming for which a solution has been developed, and, in general, any advance in the state of the art. This chapter seeks to promote an awareness of the possibilities and thereby enable an innovator to frame or cast his or her innovation as a patentable invention. With such an awareness, multiple approaches to novelty and nonobviousness can often be drawn from single innovations.

Chapter 7

Freedom to Operate

A critical inquiry in assessing the value of a product (or service) line is freedom to operate, i.e., the ability to conduct business in that product line without risk of patent infringement liability. This is one of the two major areas of investigation in a due diligence review, and any unresolved doubts can terminate or block a merger, acquisition, joint venture, investment, or any transaction whose value depends at least in part on the value of the product line. Due diligence is not in itself a determination of freedom to operate, but any due diligence review will ask whether freedom to operate has been investigated and, if so, the extent of the investigation and the conclusions drawn. Where freedom to operate has not been investigated, the due diligence review will typically be extended to include a freedom-to-operate search and review. Even where freedom to operate has been investigated, doubts can be raised if the investigation was conducted far in the past or if the scope of the investigation does not reflect the current interests or product line of the company.

The typical freedom-to-operate investigation entails a significant investment in legal services, typically in excess of $10,000 and, if the investigation leads to detailed legal analyses of particular patents, as much as $50,000 or more. To justify expenditures in this range and use of the results as a basis for business decisions involving major investments, the review must be properly conducted and the results reliable and sufficiently understood by top management that any decisions ultimately made will have a sound basis. This requires a proper search, a familiarity with the content and format of the documents revealed by the search, an under-standing of the various ways that infringement liability can arise, and knowledge of the options available for resolving or removing obstacles that are revealed by the investigation.

THE SEARCH

Identifying the Reason for the Search

The first step in a freedom-to-operate investigation is the search. Effective searching begins with an understanding of freedom-to-operate searches and how they differ from searches conducted for other reasons. Included among these other reasons are a determination of the patentability of an invention, an assessment of the validity of the claims of an issued patent, and explorations of the state of the art. Searches can also be conducted simply to find the work product or technological area of endeavor of a particular individual, research group, or corporate or business entity. The reason for the search governs the choice of the documents to be searched and the manner in which the documents will be studied. Freedom-to-operate searches are directed to *patents* that are *in force* in the *jurisdictions* where the party requesting the search seeks to do business. When the jurisdiction is the United States, the search will be directed to issued U.S. patents that have not yet expired, been abandoned, or otherwise been deemed or rendered unenforceable.

When a search has already been performed for a reason other than freedom to operate, it may be necessary to re-evaluate the search results from a freedom-to-operate perspective or to perform a follow-up search specifically directed to freedom to operate. The limitations of a patentability search, for example, can be illustrated by the common scenario of an emerging technology that begins with a fundamental discovery and progresses over time through improvements and further advances. If the fundamental discovery has been patented, the patent is likely to be found in a patentability search directed to an improvement that uses the discovery while adding benefit to the discovery. If the improvement is novel and nonobvious over the patent, an analysis of the patentability search will lead to a positive conclusion for the improvement. If the patent is still in force however and has claims broad enough to encompass the improvement, the freedom-to-operate analysis will yield a negative result.

In more established technologies as well, the patentability search may be too focused to adequately cover the question of freedom to operate. As an example, consider the skin care product example in Chapter 6. In this example, vitamin A is known to be a useful component of skin care products by virtue of its antioxidant properties, and it is then discovered that combining vitamin A with lecithin improves the effectiveness of vitamin A, leading to a new skin care product containing the combination. The relevant prior art includes an early patent on skin care products with vitamin A, the patent having been applied for when the skin care attributes of vitamin A had just been discovered. The claims of the patent focus on vitamin A but utilize "comprising" terminology (as explained in Chapter 3), thereby covering any skin care product that contains vitamin A regardless of any other active ingredients present. Even though the patent claims cover the inclusion of other active ingredients, the patent may fail to disclose lecithin as one of these other ingredients; as a result the vitamin A–lecithin combination is novel. In view of the unexpected improvement that the combination offers, the combination is nonobvious as well and therefore separately patentable over the vitamin A patent. Despite its patentability, however, the combination is covered by the vitamin A patent, which therefore dominates any patent that might be obtained on the combination and interferes with freedom to operate. If a patentability search had been conducted with the purpose of determining whether the vitamin A–lecithin combination had ever been disclosed as a component of a skin care product, the search might have missed or ignored the vitamin A patent. The search would have correctly indicated that the combination was patentable, but the searcher would not have alerted the party requesting the search to a lack of freedom to operate.

Conversely, a patentability search on an invention may reveal enforceable patents that deprive the invention of patentability but not freedom to operate. This can occur when a patent discloses the invention in its specification but fails to cover the invention in its claims. The invention may for example have been disclosed in the patent for comparative purposes, the patent holder having considered that invention either not patentable or not worthy of patenting itself, as compared to the invention that is actually claimed in the patent. The comparison may also have been included to show the superiority of the invention actually claimed. Another possibility is that the claims of the patent may have originally been broad enough to cover the invention but narrowed by amendment while the application on which the patent issued was pending. Amendments to claims in a pending patent application are commonly made without corresponding amendments to the specification. A further possibility is that the disclosure may have been something that the patent holder viewed as prior art relative to the invention claimed in the patent, and of which the later inventor may have been unaware or in disagreement. The result in any of these cases would be a conclusion that the patent presents an obstacle to patentability of the invention, but no obstacle to freedom to operate the invention. Since a patentability analysis of an invention over earlier patents typically does not include analyses of the claims of the patents, a separate analysis is required. The same result occurs when a description of the invention appears in a patent that is unenforceable for reasons of having expired, been abandoned, or been declared invalid, any of which might not be evident from the patent itself.

Likewise, a freedom-to-operate search will often fail to provide complete information relevant to patentability. A product or process that is not covered by any patent claims and is therefore free to operate, for example, may be published in nonpatent prior art or in patents that are no longer in force, none of which would be reviewed in a freedom-to-operate search. Thus, in terms of patents alone, the typical patentability search will be broader than the typical freedom-to-operate search, with search results containing significant numbers of pre-grant publications from patent authorities both in the United States and abroad as well as expired patents. Even those patents that are currently in force are studied differently for searches conducted for different reasons. The difference is due to separate legal doctrines for infringement and patentability: the breadth of infringing activity covered by the claims of a patent is often affected by matters that have no bearing on questions of what is novel or not novel, obvious or nonobvious, over the descriptive content of the patent specification.

Selecting the Search Target

If a search is to be effective, the person requesting the search, the searcher, and the corporate officer making business decisions based on the search results must all have a clear understanding of both the target, i.e., what the search is looking for, and the field of search, i.e., where the search is looking for the target. Patents are not infringed by other patents, but rather by the manufacture, use, sale, offer for sale, or importation of products, or the practice of processes.

The target in a freedom-to-operate search is therefore a product or process currently offered, practiced, or proposed, not the generic class of products or processes that one seeks to patent for oneself. A definitive answer to the freedom-to-operate question thus requires a well-defined target. At times, a business enterprise contemplating an investment in a field of technology will wish to have a sense of the patent landscape in that field prior to committing to the investment. A search with a broadly defined target may indeed provide useful information of this nature, but even if the target is defined with certain highly specific parameters, a product-specific search will often be needed as a follow-up when the time comes to assess freedom to operate.

The target in a patentability search may be highly specified as well, but will typically be a feature of a product or process that is perceived as the point of novelty. Other features will accompany the point of novelty in an actual product or process but will not typically enter into the patentability search or the search analysis if they are not themselves considered novel, and yet these other features may be the reason for a lack of freedom to operate. Selection of the target can thus have a major effect on the value of the search.

Searching by Key Words

Regardless of the Web site, search engine, or other venue through which the search is performed, key words are the most prominent tool in patent searching. A proper selection of key words is thus critical to obtaining a reliable search. As a first approximation, the key words should reflect the distinguishing characteristics or critical features of the target, i.e., those that allow the target to function in the manner that gives the target its value. In cases where certain features of the target are suspected of being proprietary to, or at least considered proprietary by, an outside party, key words reflecting these features should be searched as well.

Here again, patentability and freedom to operate tend to require different approaches. To illustrate, consider the hypothetical of an electronic device that contains carbon nanotubes whose orientation in the device affects the functioning of the device. If the orientation and its effect are novel and nonobvious, the device may be patentable for this reason. If the key words used in the search are "carbon nanotubes" and a term denoting the device itself, the search results can be used both for a patentability analysis and a freedom-to-operate analysis. If, in an attempt to reduce the number of patents that one needs to review, the key words "orientation" is added to the key words "carbon nanotubes" and the term denoting the device, the search will be effective for patentability but not for freedom-to-operate, since it will exclude patents directed to carbon nanotubes in the device in general. As another example, if the target of the search is a new electrical connector for a planar array of thermoelectric modules, the key words should include not only the connector but also the thermoelectric modules and the planar array. In general, broad searching will be more effective than highly focused searching, despite the fact that the analysis of the patents produced by the search will focus on the specifics of the target.

In some cases, one will know of a particular individual or business entity that has been active in the field in which the target of the search resides. Searching for patents listing the individual as an inventor or the entity as the assignee may therefore be a useful supplement to key word searching. Likewise, when key word searching produces a large number of patents naming a particular individual, a search based on the name of the individual may produce additional patents of relevance that did not emerge in the key word search, if the individual used synonyms or equivalent terms in some cases. Business entity searching is also of value when one switches to a new source of supply for a particular component or seeks to substitute one's own ("in-house") fabricated component for one that was previously purchased. The original source of supply may have patent coverage for the component, such coverage limiting the ability of the buyer to switch to the new source or to substitute the component fabricated in-house.

IS THE PATENT IN FORCE?

A comprehensive freedom-to-operate investigation will consider both issued patents and pre-grant publications as well as published or granted foreign counterparts that might indicate that a patent has been applied for in the United States. Pre-grant publications and foreign counterparts do not themselves raise infringement liability and will not provide definitive answers to the freedom-to-operate question. They may be of value, however, in alerting the searcher of the possibility of enforceable patents emerging in the future and may therefore justify a periodic renewal of the search to determine if and when the patents issue and what they cover when they do.

The primary focus of a freedom-to-operate investigation will be U.S. patents. Differentiating a U.S. patent from a pre-grant publication is relatively simple, since, despite similarities in appearance, each is explicitly identified as one or the other at the top of its cover page. Determining whether a patent is still in force, however, is not as simple. Four factors enter into this determination—(a) the basic term of the patent, (b) extensions to the basic term as of right to the patent holder, (c) truncations of the basic term by affirmative action of the patent holder prior to issuance, and (d) loss of enforceability of the patent by actions after its issuance. Information for determination of the first three is found on the cover page of the patent itself; one must look beyond the patent for the fourth.

The Basic Term

When one asks about the term of a patent, one is generally asking what the expiration date is. Expiration date determinations are often complex tasks, owing to changes in the law that became effective in 1995 and in the years following, and to grandfather clauses addressed to patents that were applied for before the changes went into effect.

The starting point in determining the expiration date is the date that can be referred to as the basic expiration date, i.e., the date prior to adjustments. A summary of the rule for determining the basic expiration date is as follows: for a patent issuing on an application filed on or after June 8, 1995, the basic expiration date is twenty years from the filing date, while for a patent issuing on an application filed before June 8, 1995, a transitional rule applies, according to which the basic expiration date is either twenty years from the filing date or seventeen years from the issue date, whichever is later. When the patent lists more than one filing date, however, the filing date for determining whether the transitional rule applies and the filing date for calculating the twenty-year expiration date are not the same: the most recent filing date determines whether the transitional rule applies, while the earliest filing date is the date from which the twenty-year expiration date is calculated. Dates of foreign priority applications and U.S. provisional applications are not considered in the determination of the earliest filing date.

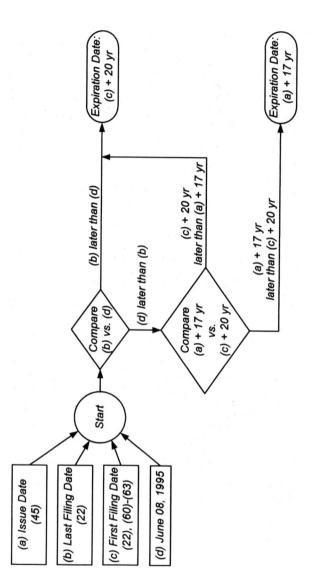

Figure 7.1. Decision Tree for Basic U.S. Patent Term

The date comparisons involved in a determination of the basic expiration date are best understood by the decision tree of Figure 7.1. Four dates serve as the input data for the decision tree, and all of the dates other than the transition date of June 8, 1995, appear on the front page of the patent, where they are identified both by words and by the INID codes (see Chapter 5). These dates are (a) the issue date (code 45), (b) the last filing date (code 22), and (c) the earliest filing date (codes 60–63). Either of the two filing dates may be a PCT filing date, but neither will be the filing date of a provisional application or a foreign priority application. The initial query in the tree is: Is the *last* filing date later than June 8, 1995? If so, the expiration date is twenty years from the *earliest* filing date. If the *last* filing date predates June 8, 1995, the transitional rule applies, whereby two dates are compared to determine which is later: seventeen years from the issue date versus twenty years from the *earliest* filing date. The later of the two is the basic expiration date.

Examples of basic expiration date determinations with varying results are shown in Figures 7.2, 7.3, and 7.4.

In Patent No. 6,453,208 (Figure 7.2), the most recent filing date as identified by code 22 is January 11, 2001, and earlier filing dates are listed under "Related U.S. Application Data" (code 63) and "Foreign Application Priority Data" (code 30). Of the earlier filing dates, only those listed under "Related U.S. Application Data" (code 63) are considered, and the earliest of these is November 8, 1994. Since the most recent filing date (January 11, 2005) is subsequent to June 8, 1995, the transitional rule does not apply, and the basic expiration date is twenty years from November 8, 1994, or November 8, 2014. The term of the patent prior to adjustment (discussed below) is measured from the issue date to the basic expiration date, or twelve years, fifty days.

In Patent No. 6,057,150 (Figure 7.3), the most recent filing date is September 18, 1998 (code 22), and although an earlier filing date is shown under "Related U.S. Application Data" (code 60), the earlier filing date is that of a provisional patent application. Since provisional applications do not enter into the calculation of the twenty-year expiration date, the filing date of September 18, 1998, governs both determinations, i.e., whether or not the transitional rule applies, and the determination of the basic expiration date. Since the filing date is subsequent to June 8, 1995, the transitional rule does not apply, and the basic expiration date is twenty years from the filing date, or September 18, 2018. The term of the patent prior to

US006453208B2

(12) **United States Patent**
Miyasaka et al.

(10) **Patent No.:** **US 6,453,208 B2**
(45) **Date of Patent:** *Sep. 17, 2002

(54) **PRINTING APPARATUS WITH REAL-TIME ERROR RECOVERY**

(75) Inventors: **Masayo Miyasaka; Takuya Hyonaga; Takaaki Akiyama; Naohiko Koakutsu; Mitsuaki Teradaira,** all of Suwa (JP)

(73) Assignee: **Seiko Epson Corporation,** Tokyo (JP)

(*) Notice: Subject to any disclaimer, the term of this patent is extended or adjusted under 35 U.S.C. 154(b) by 0 days.

This patent is subject to a terminal disclaimer.

(21) Appl. No.: **09/758,190**

(22) Filed: **Jan. 11, 2001**

Related U.S. Application Data

(63) Continuation of application No. 09/361,914, filed on Jul. 27, 1999, now Pat. No. 6,208,906, which is a division of application No. 08/730,694, filed on Oct. 11, 1996, now abandoned, which is a continuation-in-part of application No. 08/335,604, filed on Nov. 8, 1994, now Pat. No. 5,594,653.

(30) **Foreign Application Priority Data**

Nov. 8, 1993	(JP)	....	5-278637
Nov. 8, 1993	(JP)	....	5-278638
Nov. 8, 1993	(JP)	....	5-278639
Oct. 13, 1995	(JP)	....	7-265881

(51) **Int. Cl.^{7}** **G05B 9/02**
(52) **U.S. Cl.** **700/79;** 700/21; 714/2
(58) **Field of Search** 700/1, 9, 11, 27, 700/79, 213, 219, 222; 705/21; 714/1, 2; 399/7–9, 18, 19

(56) **References Cited**

U.S. PATENT DOCUMENTS

4,396,976 A	8/1983	Hyatt
4,438,507 A	3/1984	Nakajima
4,452,136 A	6/1984	Boynton et al.
4,454,575 A	6/1984	Bushaw et al.
4,745,602 A	5/1988	Morrell
4,877,345 A	10/1989	Hori
4,943,936 A	7/1990	Hirai et al.
4,989,163 A	1/1991	Kawamata et al.
4,991,972 A	2/1991	Ikenoue et al.
5,088,033 A	2/1992	Binkley et al.
5,124,809 A	6/1992	Koishikawa
5,398,305 A	3/1995	Yawata et al.
5,412,779 A	5/1995	Motoyama
5,418,891 A	5/1995	Yang
5,428,714 A	6/1995	Yawata et al.
5,507,003 A	4/1996	Pipkins
5,594,653 A	1/1997	Akiyama et al.
5,706,411 A	1/1998	McCormick et al.
5,720,015 A	2/1998	Martin et al.
6,208,906 B1 *	3/2001	Miyasaka et al. 700/79

FOREIGN PATENT DOCUMENTS

DE	38 11 661	10/1988
EP	0 470 782	2/1992
JP	61-9723	1/1986
JP	61-175816	8/1986
JP	63-21178	1/1988
JP	63-175918	7/1988
JP	1-302453	12/1989
WO	82/01609	5/1982

* cited by examiner

Primary Examiner—Paul P. Gordon
(74) *Attorney, Agent, or Firm*—Mark P. Watson

(57) **ABSTRACT**

A printing apparatus comprises a real-time command detector connected to the data receiver without the memory therebetween to detect control commands. An error recovery controller enables the printing apparatus to recover from an error state in accordance with predetermined command data detected by the command detector.

10 Claims, 18 Drawing Sheets

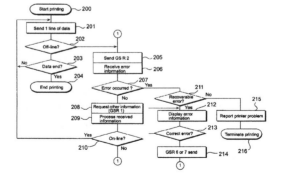

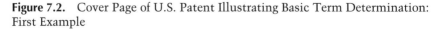

Figure 7.2. Cover Page of U.S. Patent Illustrating Basic Term Determination: First Example

112

US006057150A

United States Patent [19]

Lee et al.

[11] Patent Number: 6,057,150

[45] Date of Patent: May 2, 2000

[54] **BIAXIAL STRAIN SYSTEM FOR CULTURED CELLS**

[75] Inventors: **Ann A. Lee,** San Clemente; **Jessie Carolyn Laib,** Pinole, both of Calif.

[73] Assignee: **Bio-Rad Laboratories, Inc.,** Hercules, Calif.

[21] Appl. No.: **09/156,769**

[22] Filed: **Sep. 18, 1998**

Related U.S. Application Data

[60] Provisional application No. 60/059,396, Sep. 19, 1997.

[51] **Int. Cl.⁷** **C12M 3/04**
[52] **U.S. Cl.** **435/288.3;** 435/288.4; 435/305.1; 435/305.2; 435/297.5
[58] **Field of Search** 435/288.3, 288.4, 435/297.5, 305.1, 305.4; 29/DIG. 42; 425/DIG. 53; 38/102, 102.1, 102.2, 102.3, 102.4, 102.6, 102.8; 69/19.1–19.3; 73/788, 826, 38, 40

[56] **References Cited**

U.S. PATENT DOCUMENTS

173,720	2/1876	Guerin .
3,422,669	1/1969	Craft .
4,357,869	11/1982	Wadstein .
4,839,280	6/1989	Banes .
4,851,354	7/1989	Winston et al. .
5,073,482	12/1991	Goldstein .
5,153,136	10/1992	Vandenburgh .
5,348,879	9/1994	Shaprio et al. .
5,406,853	4/1995	Lintilhac et al. .
5,451,524	9/1995	Coble et al. .
5,686,303	11/1997	Korman .

OTHER PUBLICATIONS

N. Caille et al. *Annals of Biomedical Engineering* (1998) 26: 409–416.
J.A. Gilbert et al. *J. Biomech.* (Sep. 1994) 27(9): 1169–77.
S.R.P. Gudi et al. *Am. J. Physiol.* 274: (*Cell Physiol.* 43:) (1998) C1424–1428.

C.T. Hung et al. *J. Biomechanics* (1994) 27(2): 227–232.
A.A. Lee et al. *Am J. Physiol.* 271 (Cell Physiol. 40) (1996) C1400–C1408.
M. Liu et al. *Am. J. Physiol.* 263 (*Lung Cell. Mol. Physiol.* 7) (1992) L376–L383.
D.A. MacKenna et al. *J. Clin. Invest.* (Jan. 1998) 101(2): 301–310.
J.I. Schaffer et al. *Journal of Orthopaedic Research* (1994) 12: 709–719.
M. Sotoudeh et al. *Annals of Biomedical Engineering* (1998) 26: 1–9.
J.L. Williams et al. *Journal of Biomechanical Engineering* (Aug. 1992) 114: 377–384.
F.K. Winston et al. *J. Applied Physiol.* (1989) 67(1): 397–405.
"New Products Information Packet," Flexcell International Corp., McKeesport, PA (no date provided).

Primary Examiner—William H. Beisner
Attorney, Agent, or Firm—Townsend and Townsend and Crew LLP

[57] **ABSTRACT**

Biological cells plated on an elastic membrane are placed under biaxial strain for purposes of observation by a device that includes a support with an opening over which the membrane is secured, a movable cylinder coaxial with the opening and fitting closely but movably within the opening, and an actuating member that stabilizes and controls the position of the cylinder relative to the opening. The actuating member is coupled to the support by a threaded connection while engaging the movable cylinder. The degree of membrane stretch is accurately controlled by the rotation of the actuating member.

14 Claims, 16 Drawing Sheets

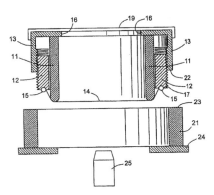

Figure 7.3. Cover Page of U.S. Patent Illustrating Basic Term Determination: Second Example

113

US005556611A

United States Patent [19]

Biesalski

[11] Patent Number: 5,556,611

[45] Date of Patent: Sep. 17, 1996

[54] **VITAMIN A AEROSOL-INHALANT PREPARATIONS AND METHOD**

[75] Inventor: **Hans K. Biesalski**, Albig, Germany

[73] Assignee: **Hermes Fabrik pharmazeutischer Praparate**, Grosshesselohe, Germany

[21] Appl. No.: **426,344**

[22] Filed: **Apr. 21, 1995**

Related U.S. Application Data

[60] Continuation of Ser. No. 839,547, Feb. 19, 1992, abandoned, which is a division of Ser. No. 346,439, May 2, 1989, Pat. No. 5,112,598.

[51] Int. Cl.^{6} **A61L 9/04; A61K 9/14; A01N 31/04**

[52] U.S. Cl. **424/46; 424/45; 514/725**

[58] Field of Search 424/45, 46; 514/725

[56] **References Cited**

U.S. PATENT DOCUMENTS

5,112,598   5/1992 Biesalski 424/46

OTHER PUBLICATIONS

H. K. Biesalski, et al. Biochemical, Morphological, and Functional Aspects of Systemic and Local Vitamin A Deficiency in the Respiratory Tract. Sep. 30, 1992. vol. 669. Ann NY Acad. Sci. pp. 325–331.

Biesalski, H. K., "Effects of intra–tracheal application of vitamin A on concentrations of retinol derivatives in plasma, lungs and selected tissues of rats," *Int. J. Vit. Nutr. Res.* (in press).

Biesalski, H. K., et al., "Bioavailability of inhalative application of vitamin A. Comparison with intramuscular and oral. administration," Bioavailability 93, Schlemmer, U. (ed.), BfE 336–345 (1993).

McDowell, E. M., et al, "Effects of viatamin A deprivation on hamster tracheal epithelium," *Virchows Arch.* (*Cell Pathol.*) 45:197–219 (1984).

Edmondson, S. W., et al. "Regulation of differentiation and keratin protein expression by vitamin A in primary cultures of hamster epithelial cells," *J. Cell Physiol.* 142:21–30 (1990).

Stofft, E., et al., "Morphological changes in the tracheal epithelium of guinea pigs in conditions of 'marginal' vitamin A deficiency," *Int. J. Vit. Nutr. Res.* 62:134–142 (1992).

Lasnitzki, I., et al., "Prevention and reversal by a retinoid of 3,4–benzpyrene– and igarette smoke condensate–induced hyperplasia and metaplasia of rodent respiratory epithelia in organ culture," *Canc. Treat Rep.* 66:1375–1380.

McDowell, E. M., et al., "Restoration of mucociliary tracheal epithelium following deprivation of vitamin A.," *Virchows Arch.* (*Cell Pathol.*) 45:221–240 (1984).

Sommer, A., et al., "Increased mortality in children with mild vitamin A deficiency," *Lancet* 585–588 (Sep. 10, 1983).

Sommer, A., et al., "Increased risk of respiratory disease and diarrhea in children with preexisting mild vitamin A deficiency," *Am J. Clin. Nutr.* 40:1090–1095 (1984).

Sommer, A., et al., "Vitamin A supplementation and childhood mortality," *Nutrition Reviews* 45(2):48–50 (1987).

Fawzi, W. W., et al., "Vitamin A supplementation and childhood mortality: A metaanalysis," *JAMA* 269:898–903 (1993).

Milton, R. C., et al., "Mild vitamin A deficiency and childhood mobidity—an Indian expreience," *Am J. Clin. Nutr.* 46:827–829 (1987).

Pinnock, C. B., et al., "Vitamin A status of children when a history of respiratory syncytial virus infection in infancy," *Aust. Paediatr. J.* 24:286–289 (1988).

(List continued on next page.)

Primary Examiner—Carlos Azpuru
Attorney, Agent, or Firm—Townsend and Townsend and Crew LLP

[57] **ABSTRACT**

A pharmaceutical preparation consisting of retinoic acid and/or an ester of retinoic acid and/or an ester of retinol as active substances, which are present in the preparation form of aerosol, is advantageously suitable for topical treatment of mucosal diseases in man and animal.

4 Claims, 3 Drawing Sheets

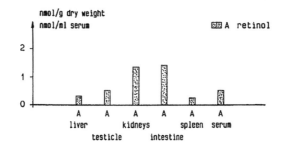

Figure 7.4. Cover Page of U.S. Patent Illustrating Basic Term Determination: Third Example

adjustment is therefore eighteen years, four months, and two weeks.

In Patent No. 5,556,611 (Figure 7.4), the most recent filing date is April 21, 1995 (code 22), and two qualifying earlier filing dates are listed under "Related U.S. Application Data" (code 60), the earliest of which is May 2, 1989. Since the most recent filing date is before June 8, 1995, the transitional rule does apply, and the basic expiration date is the later of seventeen years from the issue date and twenty years from the earliest filing date. Since the former results in the later date, the basic expiration date is September 17, 2013, and the term of the patent is exactly seventeen years.

Extensions to the Basic Term

Extensions to the patent term beyond the basic expiration date are granted by the USPTO under a variety of circumstances. One of these is when the time in which the patent is under examination at the USPTO exceeds certain limits by no fault of the patentee. Another is when the patent has been the subject of an interference, a secrecy order or an appeal (to the USPTO Board of Patent Appeals and Interferences) prior to issuance. A third is when the patent meets certain requirements set forth under the Hatch-Waxman Act. Extensions that are capable of determination prior to issuance of the patent, i.e., those not due to the Hatch-Waxman Act, are shown on the front page of the patent, typically in the left column following the word "Notice." An example is seen in Figure 7.5, depicting a patent that received an extension of 268 days.

The various extensions are calculated as follows:

Extensions Due to USPTO Delays during Examination

Delays attributable to any of the following will be result in an extension of the patent term by one day for each day of the delay:

- When more than fourteen months pass between the filing date and the first "Office Action" (rejection or allowance) from the examiner (The "filing date" in this determination is the actual filing date shown after INID code 22 unless the application is the U.S. national phase of a PCT application. In the latter case, the "filing date" in this determination is the date shown

US006653063B2

(12) **United States Patent**
Carver et al.

(10) **Patent No.:** **US 6,653,063 B2**
(45) **Date of Patent:** **Nov. 25, 2003**

(54) **HEMATOLOGY COMPOSITION USING PRESERVED WHITE BLOOD CELLS IN COMBINATION WITH SOURCE PARTICLES TO SIMULATE NATIVE WHITE BLOOD CELLS AND METHOD OF MAKING SAME**

(75) Inventors: **Frank J. Carver**, Marco Island, FL (US); **James D. Lapicola**, Pleasant Hill, CA (US)

(73) Assignee: **Hematronix, Inc.**, Plano, TX (US)

(*) Notice: Subject to any disclaimer, the term of this patent is extended or adjusted under 35 U.S.C. 154(b) by 268 days.

(21) Appl. No.: **09/877,709**

(22) Filed: **Jun. 8, 2001**

(65) **Prior Publication Data**

US 2002/0022269 A1 Feb. 21, 2002

Related U.S. Application Data

(60) Provisional application No. 60/210,918, filed on Jun. 12, 2000.

(51) Int. Cl.[7] A61K 35/78
(52) U.S. Cl. 435/2; 424/532; 424/533; 424/534; 424/725; 424/778
(58) Field of Search 435/2; 424/532, 424/533, 534, 725, 778

(56) **References Cited**

U.S. PATENT DOCUMENTS

3,873,467 A	3/1975	Hunt
3,977,995 A	8/1976	Louderback et al.
4,704,364 A	11/1987	Carver et al.
4,791,355 A	12/1988	Coulter et al.
5,380,644 A	1/1995	Yonkoski et al.
5,512,485 A	4/1996	Young et al.
5,672,474 A	9/1997	Ryan
5,858,790 A	1/1999	Kim et al.
5,902,584 A	5/1999	Nicholson et al.
6,146,901 A	11/2000	Carver et al.

Primary Examiner—Jean C. Witz
(74) *Attorney, Agent, or Firm*—J. David Wharton; Stinson Morrison Hecker LLP

(57) **ABSTRACT**

A hematology control composition and method of making the composition is provided. The control employs a plurality of components including a synthetic plasma component, a red blood cell component, a platelet component and a leukocyte component. The leukocyte component includes at least one subpopulation having particles derived from other than white blood cells.

6 Claims, No Drawings

Figure 7.5. Cover Page of U.S. Patent Illustrating Extension of Basic Term

after INID code 86 and indicated as the "§ 371 (c)(1), (2), (4) date.")

• When more than four months pass between a response to the first Office Action on the inventor's behalf and a reply by the USPTO to the response

• When more than four months pass between a successful appeal (discussed further below), i.e., a decision by the Board in the applicant's favor, and an action by the examiner implementing the decision

• When more than four months pass between the payment of the issue fee and the issuance of the patent

• When more than three years pass between the filing date (as above, the date following INID code 22 unless a later date is shown following INID code 86) and the issue date

Extensions due to any of these delays can be diminished if the inventor (or the inventor's representative) has obtained an extension of time to meet a deadline before the USPTO.

Extensions Due to Interferences,
Secrecy Orders, and Appeals

Interferences. An interference is an adversarial proceeding conducted within the USPTO between competing parties who have independently invented the same invention and who both seek to obtain a patent on the invention. Interferences are argued before and decided by the USPTO Board of Patent Appeals and Interferences and often approach lawsuits in their complexity, cost, and duration. For pending patent applications, the duration can consume a considerable portion of the time between filing and issuance, and the extension compensates for this by adding a length of time to the patent term equal to the length of time between the declaration of the interference and its final resolution.

Secrecy Orders. Secrecy orders are issued by defense agencies of the U.S. government on patent applications that these agencies believe to contain information that may be detrimental to national security. A secrecy order does not prevent a patent application from being examined, but it will prevent publication of the application and issuance of a patent on the application while the order is in effect. Secrecy orders are issued for limited time periods but are often renewed. Once a secrecy order has expired without renewal or has been lifted by the agency that imposed it and a patent has issued, the term of the patent is extended by a length of time equal to the length of time that the order has been in effect.

Appeals. A patent applicant who is dissatisfied with the decision of an examiner in rejecting all or some of the claims of the patent application is entitled to appeal the decision to the USPTO Board of Patent Appeals and Interferences. If the appeal succeeds and the Board overturns the examiner's decision, the application is returned to the examiner for further action in accordance with the Board's findings, and, in most cases, the action will result in issuance of a patent. As mentioned above, any delay by the examiner that results in more than four months passing between the Board's decision and the examiner's action will be added to the patent term. Whether or not such a delay occurs, an extension will also be granted for the duration of the appeal itself, equal to the length of time between the initiation of the appeal and the Board's decision.

Extensions Due to Patent Term Restoration
under the Hatch-Waxman Act

The Hatch-Waxman Act (whose official title is "The Drug Price Competition and Patent Restoration Act" and its later supplement "The Generic Animal Drug and Patent Term Restoration Act") provides extensions of the patent term for inventions relating to products that are required to obtain regulatory approval before being sold. These products include new drugs, antibiotic drugs, human biological products, food or color additives, medical devices, animal drugs, and veterinary biological products. The extension is designed to compensate the patent owner for the length of time that the patent owner had to await government approval before selling the product. Compensation is not complete, and the amount of extension requires knowledge of the time consumed by product testing and the time spent under review by the regulatory agency. In general, the extension is equal to one-half the time consumed by clinical testing after the application to the regulatory agency, plus all of the time spent in regulatory review, to a maximum of five years, provided that the expiration date is not extended beyond fourteen years from the date of approval. The extension is available only for the first commercial use of the drug and applies only to patent coverage on the drug itself rather than to the patent as a whole. Other drugs or inventions claimed in the same patent are covered only up to the expiration date prior to any extension due to the Hatch-Waxman Act.

Truncations of the Term by the Patent Holder

In some cases, the front page of a patent will state that the patent is subject to a "terminal disclaimer." When present, the statement appears in the left column of the front page, without an INID code. A patent bearing this indication is shown in Figure 7.6.

Note that an asterisk also appears in Figure 7.6 next to the issue date to direct the reader to the asterisk and statement in the left column. A terminal disclaimer is a document that appears in the official file of the patent at the USPTO, and, in many cases, the document shortens the term of enforceability of the patent by the

US006453250B1

(12) **United States Patent**
Andersson et al.

(10) Patent No.: **US 6,453,250 B1**
(45) Date of Patent: *Sep. 17, 2002

(54) **METHOD AND APPARATUS FOR DETECTION OF MISSING PULSES FROM A PULSE TRAIN**

(75) Inventors: **Claes Georg Andersson**, Berkeley; **Bradley R. Lewis**, Gilroy, both of CA (US); **Charles N. Villa**, Greensboro, NC (US)

(73) Assignee: **Snap On Technologies, Inc.**, Lincolnshire, IL (US)

(*) Notice: Subject to any disclaimer, the term of this patent is extended or adjusted under 35 U.S.C. 154(b) by 0 days.

This patent is subject to a terminal disclaimer.

(21) Appl. No.: **09/093,473**

(22) Filed: **Jun. 8, 1998**

Related U.S. Application Data

(63) Continuation of application No. 08/599,772, filed on Feb. 12, 1996, now Pat. No. 5,764,524.

(51) Int. Cl.^{7} G01R 23/00
(52) U.S. Cl. **702/66**; 702/67; 702/75; 377/16; 377/19; 377/20
(58) Field of Search .... 702/66, 57–59, 702/67–71, 73–78, 79, 69, 89, 106, 124–126, 176–180, 182–185, 187, 189, 190, 193, 197, 198, FOR 103, FOR 104, FOR 134, FOR 106–FOR 110, FOR 135, FOR 136, FOR 139, FOR 154, FOR 164, FOR 168, FOR 170, FOR 171; 377/28, 15–17, 19, 20; 327/18–21; 324/76.11, 12.16, 76.15, 19, 24, 76.38, 39.41, 76.42, 47.48, 76.55, 58.62, 76.74, 82, 394; 345/134, 135, 440

(56) **References Cited**

U.S. PATENT DOCUMENTS

4,142,159 A * 2/1979 Ingram et al. 327/21

4,553,426 A	*	11/1985	Capurka	327/21
4,628,269 A		12/1986	Hunninghaus et al.	327/20
4,661,778 A		4/1987	Anderson	324/380
4,670,711 A		6/1987	Daniels	324/76.16
4,804,921 A	*	2/1989	Putrow et al.	324/394
4,845,608 A		7/1989	Gdula	700/46
5,128,973 A		7/1992	Sasaki et al.	377/28
5,155,431 A	*	10/1992	Holcomb	702/68
5,198,750 A		3/1993	Prokin	324/76.47
5,202,682 A	*	4/1993	Finger	324/76.12
5,233,545 A		8/1993	Ho et al.	702/180
5,289,500 A	*	2/1994	Inou et al.	324/76.12
5,359,533 A	*	10/1994	Ricka et al.	324/76.47
5,471,402 A		11/1995	Owen	702/76
5,493,515 A		2/1996	Batchelder et al.	702/67
5,495,168 A		2/1996	de Vries	324/121 R
5,764,524 A		6/1998	Andersson et al.	702/79

FOREIGN PATENT DOCUMENTS

| EP | 0 477 507 A | 4/1992 |
| FR | 2 393 470 A | 12/1978 |

* cited by examiner

Primary Examiner—Hal Wachsman
(74) *Attorney, Agent, or Firm*—Cook, Alex, McFarron, Manzo, Cummings & Mehler, Ltd.

(57) **ABSTRACT**

A method and apparatus for detection of missing pulses from a repetitive pulse train including signal detection circuits for capturing the rising and/or falling edges of an input signal, time-stamping the captured edges, calculating the maximum and minimum instantaneous frequency over a specified time period, and displaying such frequency values. Instantaneous frequency values between any two adjacent edges are calculated based upon the time-stamps of the edges. The instantaneous frequency values in a specified time period are then sorted to find the minimum and maximum frequency values for that time period. These instantaneous frequency values are displayed in the form of a histogram evidencing the occurrence or lack of occurrence of missing pulses from the input signal.

34 Claims, 3 Drawing Sheets

```
┌─────────────────────┐
│  CONDITION INPUT    │
│      SIGNAL         │
└─────────────────────┘
           │
┌─────────────────────┐
│ DETECT CONDITIONED  │
│    INPUT SIGNAL     │
└─────────────────────┘
           │
┌─────────────────────┐
│     CALCULATE       │
│    TIME LAPSES      │
└─────────────────────┘
           │
┌─────────────────────┐
│ CALCULATE AND COMPARE│
│  FREQUENCY VALUES   │
└─────────────────────┘
           │
┌─────────────────────┐
│ COMPARE REPRESENTATIVE│
│  FREQUENCY VALUES   │
└─────────────────────┘
```

Figure 7.6. Cover Page of U.S. Patent Illustrating Truncation of Basic Term by Terminal Disclaimer

patentee itself *disclaiming* a portion of the term at the *end* of the term, hence the name "terminal disclaimer." The degree to which the term is shortened is not stated on the front page of the patent or at any other location within the patent, but can only be determined from the terminal disclaimer itself, which is publicly available from the patent file.

Terminal disclaimers are a means of overcoming certain types of rejections while the patent is pending (or obstacles to validity after the patent issues), namely rejections over other patents or applications owned by the same party that claim the same invention or an invention that is deemed to be too similar to justify a separate patent on each one. Rejections of this type are termed "double patenting," and the effect of the disclaimer is twofold: (1) to cause both patents to expire on the same date, and (2) to require that the two patents remain commonly owned by declaring that if title to one is ever transferred without the other, both will lose enforceability. These effects in combination give the patents the enforceability attribute of a single patent, thereby removing the "double patenting" aspect. In cases where one of the patents claims a filing date benefit from the other and neither was filed prior to June 8, 1995, the requirement that the patents expire on the same date is redundant since they already have a common expiration date. Nevertheless, the front page will simply indicate that the patent is subject to a terminal disclaimer, and one must review the disclaimer itself to determine whether the result is an actual truncation of the patent term.

The words "terminal disclaimer" are carried over from times when all patents were enforceable for seventeen years from their issue dates, and any such disclaimer resulted in a shortening of the term. The placement of an asterisk next to the issue date to call attention to a terminal disclaimer may also be a carry-over, since for most patents currently in force the issue date is no longer relevant to the term.

Loss of Enforceability Subsequent to Issuance

The front page of the patent indicates actions occurring prior to the issuance of a patent that affect its term of enforceability. Actions occurring subsequent to the issuance are not indicated on the front page and, in some cases, are determinable from documents in the official file. Still others require information apart from that in the patent or its file. Prominent among actions not typically recorded in the patent file are the failure to pay maintenance fees, which are required for payment to the USPTO to maintain the enforceability of a patent. The fees are due 3.5 years, 7 years, and 10.5 years after the issue date. The failure to pay a maintenance fee can be a voluntary act on the part of a patentee or an error of omission. Information as to whether maintenance fees have been paid is available to the public from the USPTO Web site.

Litigation involving a patent may also result in invalidity or unenforceability of the patent by a judicial decision. This information is readily determined by common litigation searching methods.

Overview

The sections above demonstrate that the determination of whether a patent is still in force can require considerably more than a simple look at the front page of a patent and its maintenance fee payment history on the USPTO Web site. When the services of a professional searcher are used, the searcher will not perform a full investigation of the factors that determine the expiration date, but will instead follow a conservative approach by focusing on patents whose issue dates are recent enough to indicate that the patents are not clearly expired. Any individual performing a search for the individual's own purposes should take the same approach. Actual determinations of expiration dates (or any other reason for a termination of enforceability) will then be performed by the patent attorney evaluating the search results.

RESOLVING OR REMOVING OBSTACLES

Clearing the Way by Operating
Outside the Scope of Claims

Either the expiration date or the scope of the claims can be the determinative factor in concluding that a patent presents no risk, or at most a negligible risk, of infringement liability, thereby clearing the way to freedom to operate. While the expiration date is a factual determination made by investigating and comparing dates, however, the scope of the claims is a legal determination governed by principles of law. In most cases, therefore, determining whether (or when) the expiration date has passed, despite its complexities, is a simpler task than determining whether the claims of the patent are broad enough to cover a particular commercial activity.

A preliminary screening will identify any patents that cannot be clearly or immediately eliminated on the basis of the scopes of their claims and that therefore require a legal analysis. The analysis itself is a detailed review performed on a claim-by-claim basis, a positive result being one that concludes that no valid claims are infringed, and thus no liability is presented. "No valid claims are infringed" means that each claim is deemed either not infringed or not valid over prior art despite having been allowed by the USPTO. As illustrated in Chapter 4, the approach to a complex claim set for an infringement analysis differs from the approach for a validity analysis. Both analyses however typically include a review not only of the claims and the patent as a whole but also of the "Office actions" (rejections from the examiner) and the arguments and other information submitted on behalf of the patentee in response to the Office actions, all of which are included in the official record. In the analyses, various legal doctrines are applied to this information, each doctrine representing a balancing of legal theories and considerations, with certain doctrines applicable to infringement and others to validity. The result is often a confidential document of considerable length and complexity, but when properly rendered one that will provide a sound legal basis for any commercial activity or transaction that depends on freedom to operate.

While legal doctrines are the province of a legal professional, the basic parameters of infringement are readily understood by corporate management, and an understanding of these parameters will assist management in evaluating any risks associated with bringing a product to market, expanding the market for a product, or entering new markets. As a threshold matter, U.S. patents are infringed by activities occurring within the geographic boundaries of the United States, its territories, and possessions while the patent is in force. Nevertheless, certain activities within these boundaries that would not constitute infringement in isolation become infringing activities when performed in conjunction with activities performed outside these boundaries. Further, parties that are not performing infringing activities can be liable because of the activities of others, regardless of where these activities are performed. The various liabilities can be placed under three generic, although overlapping, classes—(1) direct infringement, (2) indirect infringement established by activities in the United States alone (understood herein to include territories and possessions of the United States), and (3) indirect infringement established by activities in the United States coordinated with activities abroad.

Direct Infringement

It will be recalled from Chapter 3 that a patent claim is a recitation of "limitations," or lines of demarcation that differentiate infringing activity from noninfringing activity. Direct infringement of any claim occurs when every limitation of the claim, i.e., every feature, characteristic, or parameter that the claim recites, is met, either literally or as an equivalent, by a single party. Claims that are directed to objects, tangible or intangible, rather than to methods of manufacturing, assembling, using, treating, transforming, or otherwise acting upon an object, are infringed by making, using, offering to sell, or selling the object within the United States, or importing the object into the United States. Note that an offer for sale can constitute infringement regardless of whether the offeror itself has engaged in any of the other infringing activities, including the sale itself, and regardless of whether the sale actually occurs. Also note that importation of a patented invention is an act of infringement by itself, regardless of whether the importer sells or uses the invention. Claims directed to actions, which are typically expressed as "method" or "process" claims, are infringed by one performing the action.

Exceptions exist that result in an expansion of the scope of infringing activities in some cases and a reduction in others. Both types of exceptions occur in the medical field. The expansions arise from certain provisions of the Hatch-Waxman Act referenced above that relate to patents that claim drugs or that claim therapeutic treatments that involve the use of drugs. These provisions relate to Abbreviated New Drug Applications (ANDAs) submitted to the Federal Food and Drug Administration (FDA), and their effect is to expand the scope of infringing activities to include the submission itself of an ANDA. An ANDA is generally required for marketing approval of any new formulation of a previously approved drug or for any change to the drug or to the manner in which the drug is manufactured. Generic drug manufacturers must therefore obtain FDA approval through an ANDA before marketing a generic drug.

The provisions of the Act that define the submission of the ANDA as an act of patent infringement, together with other provisions of the Act that require the ANDA to list all relevant patents and to certify that the patent holders have been notified of the ANDA, collectively provide a means by which patent disputes involving generic drugs can be resolved in an expedited manner before the drugs are marketed.

Exceptions in the form of reductions in the scope of infringing activities apply to patents that claim medical or surgical procedures. Specifically, patent holders are denied the right to claim infringement of these patents by persons performing the procedures and, thus, claims to medical or surgical procedures are categorically unenforceable. This denial does not extend to claims for materials or objects that may be used in a procedure, such as medical devices, instruments, implants, or other articles or apparatus, or to drugs, formulations, or compositions of matter.

When addressing the claim limitations themselves, infringement analyses often turn on the meanings of the specific words used in a claim. Determinations of the meanings become complex when dictionary definitions are inappropriate or imprecise, or when the context or the record suggests that a meaning other than that in common usage was intended. Disagreements over the meanings of specific words often become major issues in patent litigation and the subject of special hearings. Nevertheless, once these issues are resolved, literal infringement of a particular claim is established when every limitation of the claim is literally met.

When it cannot be shown that every limitation is literally met, infringement can still be established by a showing that a limitation that is not literally met is met by an *equivalent*. Thus, a claim to a combination of components can be asserted over a combination that contains all but one of the components plus an equivalent to the missing component. Similarly, a claim to a multistep process can be asserted over a process in which one of the steps is replaced by an equivalent step. This ability to assert claims over equivalents is known as the "Doctrine of Equivalents." Deciding whether the Doctrine of Equivalents can be applied and to what extent is another complex legal analysis whose parameters are set forth by an extensive body of judicial decisions. The analysis involves a review of the entire record of the patent on file at the USPTO, and the factors entering into the analysis include the extent to which others in the industry consider the allegedly infringing component to be an equivalent of the claimed component; how many differences exist; how great each difference is; the effect of each difference on the functioning, operation, or overall effect of the invention; how much the invention itself differs from the prior art; and any statements or amendments included in the official record that were made in support of the patentability of the invention.

Indirect Infringement by Contributory Infringement or Inducement to Infringe

Activities that fail to meet the limitations of a patent claim or their equivalents can still give rise to infringement liability if the activities are shown to constitute contributory infringement or active inducement to infringe. These terms appear in separate subsections of the patent statute, but the two are closely related and are generally viewed as complementary expressions of an underlying theory of liability.

Contributory infringement is defined in the patent statute as the act of one who sells within the United States a component of a "machine, manufacture, combination or composition" covered by a U.S. patent or a "material or apparatus for use in practicing a patented process" covered by a U.S. patent, "constituting a material part of the invention, knowing the same to be especially made or especially adapted for use in an infringement of such patent, and not a staple article or commodity of commerce suitable for substantial noninfringing use." The statute also defines contributory infringement as the making of an offer within the United States to sell, or the importation into the United States of, a "machine, manufacture, combination or composition" that meets the above description (i.e., one that "constitutes a material part of the invention," etc.). The distinction between a component that is "a staple article of commerce suitable for substantial noninfringing use" and one that is not can be illustrated by examples from patent-related lawsuits.

One of these lawsuits involved a patent directed to oil well equipment that consisted of a combination of a string of tubing with a bypass mandrel, a retrievable gas lift valve, and a fitting for supporting the retrievable valve in the bypass mandrel (Patent No. 2,275,345). The accused infringer was a manufacturer of retrievable gas lift valves for oil wells whose customers included those who used the valves in bypass mandrels and also those who used them in mandrels that did not have bypass arrangements. Since the valve manufacturer did not itself manufacture the patented combination, the manufacturer was not a direct infringer, and valves were shown to be usable in mandrels that did not contain bypass arrangements, they were deemed to have a substantial noninfringing use. The opposite result occurred in a lawsuit involving Patent No. 4,120,570. The invention in this patent was a contact lens fabricated from a solid gas-permeable copolymer of a polysiloxanylalkyl ester and an acrylic or methacrylic ester of a monohydric alkanol. The defendant was a manufacturer of copolymers for the fabrication of contact lenses, including those specified in the patent. The defendant did not manufacture contact lenses but sold the copolymers to those who did. Evidence at trial indicated that the copolymers sold by the defendant were specially adapted for use in the manufacture of contact lenses and, at least at the time of the manufacture, had no substantial use for any purpose other than contact lenses. The existence of a noninfringing use in the gas lift valve case and the lack of noninfringing uses in the copolymer case led to the result that the manufacturer in the first case was deemed free of any infringement liability while the manufacturer in the second was held liable for contributory infringement.

Inducement to infringe is defined as the active and knowing assistance of others in committing direct infringement. Contributory infringement itself often meets this description, and the same act is often accused of constituting both contributory infringement and inducement. Inducement however covers a broader range of activities and defendants. Licensing activities, for example, even if not directed specifically to the patented invention, can lead to liability under inducement if the information supplied by the licensor includes instructions or plans which would constitute direct infringement if carried out. The design of an article whose manufacture would constitute direct infringement can render the designer liable for inducement. Actions involving repair and maintenance of a patented object or of an object used in a patented method can also lead to liability for inducement. Instructions and advertising in general can also render the instructor or advertiser liable for inducement. Inducement has also been used successfully as grounds for holding corporate officers, agents, or employees liable. Activities that are typically held not to qualify as inducement are indemnification and the mere publication of information about products or processes.

Indirect Infringement through International Commerce

While most infringement theories focus on activities performed within the United States (or its territories or possessions), U.S. patent law further provides for infringement liability under U.S. patents for certain activities that bear a connection with activities outside the United States. These provisions reflect an interest in the harmonization of U.S. patent laws with those of other jurisdictions. As described, these activities tend to overlap with activities that constitute contributory infringement and inducement to infringe, but they are set forth separately in the statute, perhaps in part to emphasize the harmonization effort. Specifically, U.S. patents that are infringed by assembling components into a combination will be infringed even when assembly occurs outside the United States if the components or a substantial portion for the components are supplied (or caused to be supplied) in or from the United States. These provisions focus on combination-type inventions that are otherwise infringed by combining components, but theories of both contributory infringement and active inducement apply.

Clearing the Way by Establishing That Claims Are Invalid

As noted above, establishing that a particular claim is invalid is an alternative to establishing that a product or process falls outside the scope of the claim—both will avoid infringement liability. In many freedom-to-operate analyses, some of the claims are deemed not infringed while the remainder are deemed to be invalid, the two conclusions collectively covering all of the claims of a patent. Some analyses conclude that particular claims are *both* not infringed *and* invalid, thereby providing two defenses against the patent owner rather than one and thus a stronger response to an allegation of infringement. Like claim scope, claim validity is a legal determination governed by principles of law, and the conclusion that a particular claim does not meet the statutory requirements of patentability despite having passed examination in the USPTO is reachable only upon a detailed legal analysis. This is true regardless of whether the conclusion is based on prior art (the most common ground) or any other reason. The choice between noninfringement and invalidity as a means of avoiding liability is not arbitrary however, since each conclusion entails its own distinct analysis and balancing of factual considerations, and an assertion of invalidity may be rebuttable by the patent owner with information that is under the patent owner's control or not available to the attorney performing the analysis. In most cases, therefore, freedom-to-operate analyses will first attempt to establish noninfringement and will attack validity only when noninfringement cannot be shown or can only be shown with less than full confidence.

A validity analysis will typically involve an independent search directed specifically to validity, which as noted above will differ from the freedom-to-operate search in terms of the materials being searched, the sources of the materials, and how the materials are read. The scope of the search may therefore go well beyond patents and traditional forms of technical literature to include information and activities of limited distribution or activities for which information is not generally accessible to the public.

Clearing the Way by Engaging Only in Nonpatentable Activities

Theoretically, one can use a freedom-to-operate search to establish that a product or process of interest is patentable to no one and thereby free for use without any risk of patent infringement liability. As discussed above, concerns over particular claims can be eliminated by showing that the claims are invalid over prior art, but showing that a product or process is prior art in an absolute sense to any patent that could still be in force (without the need to address specific patents) is a further means of establishing freedom to operate. Such a showing would mean that the party seeking to establish freedom to operate would likewise be excluded from patent protection. Any proprietary interest or rights in the technology will therefore be based on means other than patent protection, and as a result one may lack the ability to prevent competitors from competing directly by offering or practicing the same technology. Nevertheless, freedom to use the technology may have value by itself when patent protection is not obtainable for some reason, or when other forms of proprietary interest are more appropriate, or both. The ability to add a product or service may, for example, enhance the value of a product, suite of products, or service that is already offered, or enhance the market stature of a supplier, or simply add to customer good will by offering the customers a common source of supply for related products or services.

When proprietary interest for nonpatentable subject matter has a value of its own, however, the most prominent example of a nonpatent proprietary interest for functional technology is a trade secret. An advantage of a trade secret is that it can be established by contract or by mere secrecy and is therefore not subject to the subject matter, novelty, nonobviousness, and full disclosure requirements of the patent law. Another advantage is that the duration of a trade secret is not limited by statute but only by how long secrecy can be maintained or by contractual agreement. A disadvantage is that trade secrets can be extinguished by discovery of the secret by a competitor or by disclosure of the secret, whether done innocently (i.e., by one who is under no obligation to the holder of the trade secret) or in violation of an agreement. Another disadvantage is that a trade secret is violated only by those who learned the trade secret from its originator and are obligated to maintain its secrecy; trade secrets are not violated by those who derive the information independently. Technology that requires regulatory approval cannot be protected by trade secret, since the approval process typically requires disclosure that is subject to public access. Another example of a nonpatent asset is specialized skill or expertise.

To positively conclude that no patent could still be in force and cover a product or activity, one would have to establish that the product or activity was in the prior art in the form of published literature or commercial use more than one year prior to the earliest possible filing date of any patent that could still be in force. This reflects the "statutory bar" provision of the U.S. patent statute, which bars an inventor from presenting evidence of the inventor's earlier date of invention to overcome a citation of prior art when the prior art is a publication or commercial use that has occurred more than one year prior to the inventor's filing date. Since the term of a patent is subject to so many factors, however, as demonstrated above, one cannot know with certainty how far back in time one must go to establish a statutory bar to any patent that could still be in force. Nevertheless, one can conclude with a reasonable degree of confidence that any publication or commercial use that precedes the present by twenty-five years or more will eliminate the possibility that any patent covering the same subject matter can still be in force.

Clearing the Way by Obtaining a License or Assignment

There are times when infringement cannot be avoided, either at all or without causing a significant reduction in the value of a product line. In some cases as well, a company may find it beneficial to obtain rights under a patent as a means of establishing a business relationship with a patent owner or of preserving or promoting good relations with a patent owner with a view toward eventually forming such a relationship, even if the patent can be easily avoided. In still further cases, a patent may be available for license at a conveniently low rate and the possession of rights under the patent may add benefit to an already established market position. In situations such as these, a license under the patent or an assignment of the patent may be appropriate.

Patent licensing and assignments are a legal specialty that is the subject of numerous treatises and the purview of specialized practitioners. For the purposes of this book, however, a few considerations are worthy of note. An assignment, or full transfer of ownership, is typically more costly than a license, with fewer options of termination. In many cases as well, assignments are either not offered or not needed. A lesser form of transfer but one that is equivalent in certain aspects of its scope, including the ability to exclude competitors, is an exclusive license, while a nonexclusive license is an even lesser form in terms of the rights and obligations of, and the cost to, the licensee. All of these transfers, however, and licenses in particular, are capable of considerable variation in the extent of rights transferred and the obligations of the parties following transfer.

The choice between an exclusive license and a nonexclusive license will depend on the needs and expectations of the parties. A nonexclusive license is particularly favorable to the patent owner since it presents the patent owner with the possibility of obtaining licensing revenues from the patent that are multiples of the amount that can be obtained from a single licensee. A nonexclusive license may also be favorable to the licensee if it is available at lower cost than an exclusive license. A common situation in which a nonexclusive license is sufficient is one where the patent is a dominating patent and the licensee has its own patent coverage. The result is freedom to operate as well as the right to exclude competition from the licensee's proprietary technology. Other situations favoring either an exclusive or nonexclusive license will depend on the relationship between the patent owner and the licensee and their relative patent holdings, and the nature of the product line, the market, and the industry as a whole. Both exclusive and nonexclusive licenses are further useful where only limited rights are needed to provide the licensee with freedom to operate. Licenses can thus be limited to particular fields of use of the patent, or to designated geographical areas, or to limited periods of time.

MISCELLANEOUS: PUBLISHED PATENT APPLICATIONS AND PROVISIONAL RIGHTS

Patent searches conducted for any reason will typically include published patent applications ("pre-grant patent publications") as well as issued patents. In freedom-to-operate searches, a published patent application is not an actual indication of patent coverage but instead an indication that a patent has been applied for. There is no assurance that a patent will issue or has issued on the application itself or that if a patent does issue, that the claims of the patent will be the same as those appearing in the published application. When the published application appears to raise questions of patent infringement liability if it were to issue as a patent, the status of the application is readily determinable from the publicly available USPTO records, and if a patent has in fact issued on the application, the patent itself is readily identified and obtained.

Since this chapter sets forth the various forms of infringement liability, it is worth mentioning here the proprietary right that a published patent application affords its owner. Since a published patent application is not a patent, the owner of a published patent application does not have the right to exclude others from practicing the invention by virtue of the publication itself. Only when a patent issues on the application does the publication provide the owner with a right beyond those of the patent. The right conferred by the publication is termed a "provisional right" and it consists of the right to collect a "reasonable royalty" for infringing acts occurring during the period between publication and issuance. The royalty is collectible only after the patent has issued and is subject to the requirement that the infringer had actual knowledge of the published application at the time infringement began. The determination of a "reasonable" royalty is governed by the prevailing licensing rates in the industry to which the invention pertains. Once the patent issues, the owner is no longer restricted to demanding a "reasonable" royalty and may in fact refuse to allow any further practice of the invention.

Chapter 8

Patent Portfolio Referencing

The referencing scheme that the company uses to identify and differentiate the patents and patent applications in the company's portfolio is a topic of interest to middle management, patent administrators, corporate counsel for companies that do not have a patent administrator, and anyone directly involved on a day-to-day basis with the portfolio. Neither top management nor the board of directors will have such direct involvement or a need for an understanding of the referencing system. Nevertheless, both top management and the board will be aware when no such system exists and will feel the inadequacies of a system that is poorly designed or implemented, since without such a system lower management will not be able to provide ready answers to questions regarding the company's patent portfolio. The lack of an adequate system can reflect poorly on the performance of those with direct responsibility for the company's patents and reduce efficiency at all management levels in the various decision-making processes in which patents are a factor.

Patent portfolio referencing is the assignment of a reference number or code to an invention and including that code in all documents relating to that invention. Different codes are assigned to different inventions, and the system enables its users to index and track patents and patent applications; to group them by marketing division, product line, research group, or any other category that the company will find useful; to compile and present them when preparing reports, budgets, or the like; and in general to find the appropriate source for answers to any questions relating to the company's patent coverage. Any portfolio that includes more than a few inventions is likely to benefit from such a system. Referencing systems can be used both internally and externally, i.e., in communications within the company as well as communications between the company and those outside, such as vendors, competitors, marketing partners, outside counsel, and investors.

WHY A SEPARATE SYSTEM?

Reference codes are ubiquitous in business correspondence—every "Re" line in a letter has at least one, and many letters exhibit reference codes not only in the "Re" line but also after the writer's signature. For companies whose patent services are provided by outside counsel, the counsel has its own referencing system and asks its clients to use the appropriate reference code in any related communications. The company may also have a company-wide referencing system for documents and correspondence in general that is used by all of the company departments including the patent staff. Why then should the company have its own specialized referencing system for the patent portfolio?

Where a company-wide document referencing system exists, it is helpful to distinguish patent files from files for other company matters, legal or otherwise. A reference code that indicates at a glance that the code is patent-related will inform the reader that a stray memo, e-mail, fax, letter from outside the company, or any piece of communication bearing the code is likewise patent-related. This helps direct the item to the appropriate person and allows the contents of the item to be read in the proper context. Misfilings can be minimized and action items can be readily identified and acted upon.

When outside counsel is used, the company can indeed use the counsel's referencing system to distinguish documents that are patent-related from those that are not. The system used by outside counsel, however, will not generally serve the needs of the company, since these needs will differ from those of outside counsel. Outside counsel, for example, will use the system to distinguish files for one client from those for another, a distinction that will be of no use to the company since the company will typically not have documents relating to counsel's other clients unless sent in error. Conversely, the company will often need or wish to know the product line or company department or division to which a particular invention relates or from which the invention arose, a matter that is not generally of concern or interest to outside counsel. For other types of information, outside counsel and the company may both be interested but for different purposes. For example, outside counsel will use the reference code for accounting and billing purposes, which primarily reflect past activity, while the company's main interest will lie in budgeting for future activity, and the budgeting may again be product oriented or department oriented. Both outside counsel and the company will also need to know which patents or patent applications are legally related to other patents or patent applications, although outside counsel may have a greater interest or need in having the code reflect the nature of the relationship. Furthermore, either side may introduce gaps in the numbering scheme and for different reasons, with the result that a gap introduced by one may confuse the other or falsely suggest that something has been overlooked. Outside attorneys typically incorporate "matter" numbers in their reference codes to enable the attorneys to accommodate the clients' desire to have invoices segregated according to specific inventions or other items. Matters will be numbered consecutively, regardless of the type of matter, with no distinction between patents, searches, studies and legal opinions, licensing negotiations and contracts, and adversarial disputes between the client and others, even though each matter will have a distinct number. Their clients, by contrast, tend to consider opinions, licenses, and third-party disputes in association with the patents to which they refer rather than as separate matters.

With relatively small patent portfolios, the title of an invention is often a sufficient identifier for correspondence and documents in general that relate to the invention. As a portfolio grows, however, titles become less effective as means of distinction, since inventions related to a common product can be confusingly similar. Furthermore, between the time the inventor presents the invention to the attorney and the time the application is finalized and submitted to the USPTO, the title of a patent application may have been changed to more accurately reflect the invention as claimed in the application. The title may even be modified by the patent examiner while the application is pending. The inventor's original title may also have included code words, expressions, or abbreviations commonly used within the company that are inappropriate for a patent application.

CONSTRUCTING A REFERENCING SYSTEM

No universal referencing system can be devised that will serve the needs of every company. The most useful reference codes will contain several fields, however, and the following are suggestions of fields to include.

Recommended:

1. It is useful to begin each reference code with a field containing an arbitrary indicator that the document refers to a patent-related matter. Use of the company name or initials as a component of this field is not advisable since it is likely that other departments of the company will use the same name or initials in their own internal referencing systems, and the use of the name or initials by more than one department will dilute the distinction between departments while also consuming digits in the reference.

2. In addition to the patent indicator field, the reference number should contain at least two fields dedicated to the invention itself: one to indicate a particular invention and the second to distinguish among different applications or filings that arise from the invention. A brief explanation of the different filings that can result from a single invention is presented in the third section of this chapter.

3. All reference codes should contain a uniform number of digits or characters within each field and a uniform number of fields. This will reduce the likelihood of errors due to the omission of digits or characters, or the insertion of extraneous digits or characters. It will also alert the patent administrator or staff when an error is present. Reference numbers with uniform numbers of digits or characters will also be most readily compatible with databases in which the numbers, and documents bearing the numbers, are to be entered and recalled.

Optional:

1. As noted above, reference codes may reflect internal company categorizations, such as product lines or company departments or divisions. A separate field with such an indication will be

helpful in internal company accounting or expense attribution and budgeting, and will also provide a ready means for making compilations or reporting the status for all patent matters related to a product line or division.

2. A separate field that indicates the year of receipt of an invention disclosure by management or the legal or patent department of the company may also be useful, since this may help in prioritizing the patent application or in allowing management to identify items that have been on hold or neglected for long periods of time. It is recommended however that the year be represented by something other than the actual year itself so that it is not readily evident to the uninformed reader. Reasons for this are explained below under the heading "Not Recommended."

3. Reference codes may contain fields that distinguish provisional patent applications from nonprovisional patent applications. These are two of the "different applications or filings" referred to above in item (2) under the "Recommended" list, but are mentioned again here since unlike other patent applications, provisional applications have a strictly limited life span and each has a critical deadline for replacement with a nonprovisional application. A further explanation is given in the "Patent 'Families'" section of this chapter.

4. A field may also be included to indicate the country, geographical region, or patent jurisdiction in which the patent application has been filed. This is readily done with the use of two-letter codes that are universally used among various patent authorities of the world. A complete list of these codes is found in the United States Patent and Trademark Office (USPTO) Web site (www.uspto.gov). Some of the more prominent codes are listed in the table below. Further explanations of some of the entries in this table and of foreign filing in general are presented in Chapter 9 of this book.

5. If the company has a patent staff of more than one in-house patent professional (i.e., patent attorney or patent agent), the reference code may include a field that identifies the professional, such as by initials. This will facilitate routing, but is usually unnecessary except when the patent staff is large and has a large amount of correspondence with outside parties.

Code	Country	Code	Country	Code	Country
AU	Australia	FI	Finland	NL	Netherlands
BE	Belgium	FR	France	NO	Norway
BR	Brazil	GB	Great Britain	NZ	New Zealand
CA	Canada	HK	Hong Kong	PC	Patent Cooperation Treaty Application
CH	Switzerland	ID	Indonesia	RU	Russian Federation
CN	China	IE	Ireland	SA	Saudi Arabia
CZ	Czech Republic	IN	India	SE	Sweden
DE	Germany	IT	Italy	TW	Taiwan
DK	Denmark	JP	Japan	US	United States
EP	European Patent Office	KR	South Korea	ZA	South Africa
ES	Spain	MX	Mexico		

Not Recommended:

1. As noted above, the inclusion of company initials in the reference code is not recommended, since other company divisions may include the same initials in their own referencing systems. With the same initials appearing in different referencing systems, the ability to distinguish patent-related matters from other company matters is reduced.

2. As also mentioned above, a clear or uncoded date indicator is not advised. If a date (or even just the year) is readily discernible to a person from outside the company despite that person's lack of familiarity with the individual fields of the reference code and what they signify, this might provide the person with information that would otherwise be confidential. Dates are of high significance in most patent disputes, and revealing the date or year in a manner that an adversary can readily decipher can place the company at a strategic disadvantage.

PATENT "FAMILIES"

Item (2) under the above list of "Recommended" code components refers to a field that distinguishes among different patent applications arising from the invention. While the filing of multiple patent applications relating to a single invention and their relation to each other is a matter that is most often left to the patent attorney, managers will benefit from a rudimentary understanding of these different applications, and also of which applications are related and therefore not independent.

Provisional versus Nonprovisional Applications

U.S. patent law provides for the filing of provisional patent applications as a relatively inexpensive means of obtaining an officially recognized filing date that can later serve as the effective filing date of a nonprovisional patent application (i.e., a utility or, informally, a "regular" patent application). Provisional patent applications are not examined by the USPTO and do not mature into patents, and the official fee imposed by the USPTO for the filing of a provisional patent application is lower than those for utility patent applications. Since provisional patent applications do not require claims, the applications are typically prepared quickly and often without an attempt to meet the requirements as to form that a utility application must meet.

Further discussion of provisional applications appears in Chapter 11. For purposes of portfolio referencing, it is important to understand the relationship between a provisional application and its corresponding utility application. The provisional application is not a required preliminary step toward the filing of a nonprovisional application, but rather an option to one who seeks to obtain an early filing date without investing the time and expense (in both the filing fee and attorney fees) that are typically involved in the preparation and filing of a nonprovisional application. The value of a provisional application is the applicant's ability to transfer the benefit of the filing date of the provisional application to a nonprovisional application which can be filed as much as one year after the provisional. The value of an early filing date is explained in detail in Chapter 5 ("Identifying Prior Art"). Many companies therefore file provisional patent applications as a preliminary stage of applying for a patent.

Since the opportunity to file a nonprovisional application that claims the benefit of a provisional application lasts only one year from the filing of the provisional application, it is important to know which applications are provisional and which are nonprovisional. If this is evident from the reference codes, the codes can serve as one means of alerting both patent staff and management when a deadline is pending, the lapsing of which may mean a loss of patent rights.

Initial Utility Application versus
Subsequent Related Applications

Patent applications are termed "related" when they share legal benefits, notably the filing date benefit. A group of related patent applications is often called a "family," whose members are related to each other in various ways. Some related applications are filed in response to requirements imposed by the USPTO, while others are the result of strategic actions taken by the company that owns the invention or the attorney handling the application before the USPTO. While the specific relationship can vary, it is neither important nor practical that this be reflected in the reference number. Nevertheless, a rudimentary understanding of the different relationships will often be of value.

As nonprovisional applications are typically filed just under a year subsequent to the filing of provisional applications, other related applications are likewise typically filed at successive points in time. Using the "family" analogy, an application is commonly referred to as a "parent" of any subsequently filed application that claims a filing date benefit from the first application. Likewise, the terms "grandparent," "great-grandparent," etc., are also used depending on how many generations are present.

A *continuation* application is identical to its parent (although it can later be amended independently of the parent) and is filed at the initiative of the applicant (or the applicant's attorney) to obtain further opportunity to respond to or negotiate with the examiner. Continuation applications are often filed when the attorney seeks to shift to a new claiming strategy at a relatively late stage in the examination procedure and the examiner has declined, or is expected to decline, to permit such a shift in the parent application. A continuation application enjoys the full benefit of the filing date of its parent.

A *divisional* application is likewise identical to its parent but is filed in response to a requirement by the examiner that the applicant restrict the parent to a portion of the claims originally filed. The reason typically given by the examiner for this requirement is that the original set of claims covered too great a breadth of subject matter for the scope of search that the examiner was willing to perform in a single patent application. The applicant responds by electing a subset of the original claims and files the divisional to obtain examination of the remaining claims. Like a continuation application, a divisional application enjoys the full benefit of the filing date of its parent.

A *continuation-in-part* ("C-I-P") application is filed at the initiative of the applicant and is not identical to the parent but rather contains new descriptive material and possibly new or broader claims in addition to the descriptive material and claims of the parent. The "in-part" portion of the title reflects the fact that the application contains both the original material and new material. Only those claims of the C-I-P that are fully supported by descriptive material in the parent application enjoy the benefit of the parent's filing date; claims that extend beyond the scope of the descriptive material in the parent are entitled only to the filing date of the C-I-P.

A *reissue* application is filed after the issuance of a patent to modify the patent, typically by either reducing or expanding the scope of the claims. The reissue applicant must state that the original patent claimed either more or less than the applicant was entitled to claim, for any of a variety of reasons.

SAMPLE REFERENCE CODES

In designing a referencing scheme, the number and selection of fields in the reference will depend on how much the user wishes the reference to convey and to what extent the user intends to rely on the reference to differentiate among patent applications. The following are samples to illustrate the two ends of the spectrum of referencing complexity. Each of these two reference number prototypes is designed for use on all communications with the patent attorney, all internal company communications, all communications between the attorney and the USPTO, and optionally all communications between the company and outside companies or persons, that relate to a particular patent application.

At the simple end of the spectrum is the two-field prototype:

PT-001

Field 1 ("PT"): an arbitrary symbol to indicate that the item is patent-related; this symbol will appear on all documents relating to all patents and patent applications

Field 2 ("001"): a simple number to identify a particular invention and to differentiate among inventions; this number will be used on all patent applications and patents that reflect this invention or that arise from this invention

The five-field prototype shown below represents the complex end of the spectrum:

QR-CP-0034-01-US

Field 1 ("QR"): an arbitrary symbol to indicate that the item is patent-related; appearing on all documents relating to all patents and patent applications

Field 2 ("CP"): initials to indicate an internal company division to which the invention relates; for example, Consumer Products (CP), Industrial Products (IP), Specialty Products (SP), Personal Care Products (PC); alternative: initials to indicate a particular product line

Field 3 ("0034"): a numeral assigned to the invention

Field 4 ("01"): a numeral differentiating among different patent applications relating to the same invention and clearly distinguishing a provisional application from a nonprovisional application; for example, 00 may designate a provisional application; 01 may designate the first nonprovisional application claming benefit from the nonprovisional; and 02, 03, and 04 may designate related nonprovisional applications, such as continuations, divisionals, and C-I-Ps, claiming benefit from the first nonprovisional application in the order in which they were filed

Field 5 ("US"): country or jurisdiction in which the application was filed, by two-letter country or jurisdiction code

In summary, an in-house patent portfolio referencing system should be crafted with care to meet both the short-term and long-term needs of the company, with the capability to grow as the portfolio grows.

Chapter 9

Multinational Patent Filing

Very few corporations that count patents among their assets will find a patent portfolio adequate if the portfolio is limited to U.S. patents. Any corporation with divisions in Canada or Mexico or overseas, whose marketing strategy extends to these regions or that has competitors with marketing activities in these regions, will need to include foreign patent protection in its intellectual property budget. Decisions relating to foreign patent filing are ultimately the responsibility of the corporate manager, since foreign filing will have a major impact on the manager's budget, and all managers, particularly upper management, will at some point rely on the foreign patent portfolio as part of the valuation of the corporation and its product lines, or will use the foreign patents to support the corporation's competitive position.

No single patent covers the entire world. Instead, patents are granted by individual countries or regional groups of countries. When confronted with foreign filing decisions, the first questions that managers typically ask are How much will it cost? and Will the patents be worth anything, i.e., how strongly does a particular country enforce its patents? Once the manager learns that the cost can be considerable, depending on which countries are selected and how many, and that enforceability depends in large part on the corporation's ability to detect infringement abroad and its willingness to commit to the expense of litigating abroad, a number of questions arise that require more detailed answers: What international patent treaties exist and how do they affect the timing and cost of foreign filing decisions? Which if any countries limit the types of inventions on which they will grant patents? Are patent owners in these countries subject to "working requirements" and "compulsory licensing" and if so, how will this affect the exclusivity and value of a patent?

INTERNATIONAL PATENT TREATIES

A variety of international patent treaties exist, each serving a separate purpose while interrelating with the other treaties. The following are the more prominent treaties with summaries of their most relevant provisions.

The Paris Convention

The earliest concern by the international patent community for inventors seeking to apply for patents outside their native countries was the absolute novelty requirement, a widely adhered to rule that denied patents to inventions that had been known or disclosed anywhere in the world before the date on which the application had been filed. This meant that a patent application had to be actually received in the patent office of each country where coverage was sought before even a single disclosure of the invention, by the inventor or otherwise, had been made. The United States and Canada ultimately altered their patent laws to provide inventors a grace period between the disclosure or commercial use of an invention and the filing date of a patent application, and a number of other countries provide a grace period for very limited categories of disclosures, but these are exceptions. For a patent applicant seeking multinational coverage, the need to secure filing dates in all countries where patent coverage is sought before any outside disclosure of the invention imposed a difficult burden on the applicant, since each country required its own set of application papers and required the applicant to retain patent attorneys registered to practice in that country. Added to the burden was the cost imposed by both the local attorneys and the patent authorities in each country at the filing stage. The lessening of this burden was the central and most well-known provision of the "Paris Convention for the Protection of Industrial Property," commonly known as "the Paris Convention," first adopted in 1883 and revised and expanded numerous times since.

The Paris Convention addressed this issue by establishing a "right of priority" which recognizes a filing date of a patent application in one country as the filing date for corresponding patent applications filed in other countries that are signatories to the Convention. To qualify for this right, filings in the other countries must be completed within one year of the filing of the original, or "priority," application and an express claim to the right of priority must be made in each application other than the priority application. The Paris Convention thus allows an applicant to file an application in any single country and wait a full year before deciding whether and where to extend one's patent protection to other countries, while still claiming the benefit of the original filing date. Applications filed pursuant to the Convention are not invalidated by any acts of the applicant or its competitors, or by publications of any kind, occurring in the interval between the filing of the priority application and the filing of the subsequent applications. The Convention is universally used by those seeking multicountry patent protection. Academic institutions, where early filing dates are necessary for purposes of predating publications of inventions in both scientific journals and grant applications, benefit from the Convention. Industry likewise benefits, since many inventions arise at production facilities or at laboratories closely associated with production facilities and are introduced into production, disclosed in marketing literature, or displayed at industry shows or conventions soon after their discovery. Any individual or corporation seeking patent coverage in more than its country of domicile will take advantage of the Paris Convention.

As of the year 2006, there were approximately 170 signatories ("contracting states") to the Paris Convention, with certain of these having joined the Convention as late as 2005. Rights of priority under the Paris Convention extend to patent applications filed under other conventions as well; the one-year deadline can thus be met by filing an international application under the Patent Cooperation Treaty (PCT) or regional patent applications under regional conventions such as the European Patent Convention, the Eurasian Patent Convention, the Gulf Cooperation Council, the African Intellectual Property Organization, and the African Regional Industrial Property Organization, all discussed below. For this reason, the terms "jurisdictions" and "contracting states" are used rather than "countries" when referring to signatories of the Paris Convention. The same terms are likewise used in connection with other conventions. The country that is most notably absent from the contracting states of the Paris Convention is Taiwan. Despite its role in global industry and commerce, Taiwan is thus a continuing anomaly, and unwary patent applicants frequently miss the opportunity for patent coverage in Taiwan for this reason. The number of contracting states to the Convention continues to expand, however; thus, Taiwan and other countries that are not presently signatories may eventually become so.

The Patent Cooperation Treaty

A further step in the advancement of technology worldwide by assisting inventors in their international patent filings was the Patent Cooperation Treaty (PCT), first implemented in 1970 and since expanded and revised numerous times. The PCT offers its signatories additional time to make the decision whether and where to file, a consolidation of certain functions in the process of multijurisdictional patent filings, and valuable information to the applicant prior to the time when the applicant must commit to the expense of patent filings in multiple jurisdictions. An application filed pursuant to the PCT (an "international patent application") is first sent to a single Receiving Office, which is typically the national or regional patent office of the contracting state in which the applicant is domiciled (applicants based in the United States will typically use the United States Patent and Trademark Office as the Receiving Office). The filing date at the Receiving Office is then recognized as the filing date in any PCT contracting state in which the applicant may eventually decide to proceed. As noted above, the filing in the Receiving Office qualifies the application for the benefits of the Paris Convention, and can therefore be done within the one-year period following the priority application with full benefits of the filing date of the priority application.

Once the international application is filed, the application process proceeds in two phases, an "international" phase and a "national" (also referred to as "regional") phase. In the international phase, the application is under the jurisdiction of the International Bureau and the International Search Authority, each of which performs certain administrative functions with respect to the application. The International Bureau is in Geneva, Switzerland, and the applicant can designate either United States Patent and Trademark

Office, the European Patent Office, or the Canadian Intellectual Property Office as the International Search Authority. Included among the functions that the International Bureau and International Search Authority perform are a patentability search, the results of which are compiled in an International Search Report and sent to the applicant; publication of the entire application in a form available to the public; and official statements addressing the patentability of the invention, variously titled a "Written Opinion," an "International Preliminary Examination Report," and an "International Preliminary Report on Patentability."

In the national phase, the application comes under the jurisdiction of the patent offices of individual contracting states of the applicant's choice. To enter the national phase, the applicant forwards a copy of the application to the individual patent offices within a designated time period. The application undergoes further examinations in these patent offices, and if the application passes these examinations, the application will mature into national (or regional) patents.

Of the two phases, therefore, the first, or international, phase provides the applicant with a preliminary view of the prospects that the patent application will face in the second, or national, phase. The international phase also provides the applicant the option of terminating the procedure prior to the national phase, and of saving the attendant expenses, in the event that the prospects are negative or in such doubt that the applicant considers the expense unjustified.

The entry into the national phase is a major decision point in the PCT procedure for reasons of cost. Fees for national phase entry are separately imposed by each country, and will therefore be the applicant's highest costs after the attorney fees incurred in drafting the original patent application. These fees include filing fees imposed by the patent authorities in each PCT contracting state in which the applicant elects to proceed, the engagement of local attorneys for representation before the patent authorities, and, in many cases, the costs of translating the application into the language required by each contracting state. Depending on the length and complexity of the application and the selected contracting state, these costs can range from approximately $2,000 to over $10,000 per state. Additional costs are the periodic annuities that are imposed by the patent authorities to maintain the viability of a patent application or patent in their jurisdictions. The deadline for entering the national phase is determined from the earliest filing date, which in the case of applications claiming the benefit of a priority application under the Paris Convention is the filing date of the priority application. For many PCT contracting states, the deadline is thirty months from this date. Failure to meet the deadline generally results in a loss of potential patent rights in those countries.

As in the Paris Convention, the contracting states of the PCT include regional groups of countries as well as individual countries. The number of individual countries that are contracting states to the PCT, either on their own or through a regional patent treaty, is approximately 130, with Taiwan again as a notable exception. Other notable exceptions are Argentina, Bolivia, Venezuela, Chile, Peru, and Kuwait. As in the Paris Convention, however, the number of exceptions tends to decrease each year as further countries join the PCT.

The European Patent Convention

The European Patent Convention created the European Patent Office (EPO), which is located in Munich, Germany, and is empowered by European countries that are signatories to the Convention to examine patent applications and grant patents. Once a European patent is granted, the applicant can validate the patent in individual European countries at the choice of the patentee and thereby obtain a series of national patents that are enforceable in those countries. The applicant has two opportunities to decide which European countries the patent will cover—first, upon filing the application at the EPO, and second, after the grant of the European patent. The filing fee at the application stage increases incrementally with each designated country up to seven countries, with no further increase for additional countries. Validation is limited to the countries designated at filing but can be limited further upon grant at the option of the applicant.

A European application receives a single and thorough examination by the EPO, and the result of the examination is accepted by all countries designated in the application. Certain European countries are not equipped to perform examinations on their own; therefore, EPO is the only means by which these counties can obtain a proper examination. Furthermore, while many European countries are capable of issuing patents independently, a significant number will only issue patents by validating a granted EPO application. Validation decisions need only be made after the EPO application is granted, and since the costs of validation are imposed by each country on an individual basis, a common means of cost management is to designate all of the EPO contracting states upon filing, and postpone specific decisions until the time of validation, which can be several years later.

Like the Paris Convention and the PCT, the European Patent Convention is an evolving and adaptable agreement. As of 2006, the contracting states are as follows:

Austria	Hungary	Poland
Belgium	Iceland	Portugal
Bulgaria	Ireland	Romania
Cyprus	Italy	Slovak Republic
Czech Republic	Latvia	Slovenia
Denmark	Lithuania	Spain
Estonia	Luxembourg	Sweden
Finland	Malta	Switzerland/Liechtenstein
France	Monaco	Turkey
Germany	Netherlands	United Kingdom
Greece		

Additional countries that are not signatories to the Convention but nevertheless recognize European patents if designated when the application is filed are the "extension countries": Albania, Macedonia, Croatia, Serbia, Montenegro, Bosnia, and Herzegovina.

The Eurasian Patent Convention

The Eurasian Patent Convention grants patents that are recognized by and enforceable in its member countries, which are the Russian Federation, Turkmenistan, Belarus, Tajikistan, the Republic of Kazakhstan, the Republic of Azerbaijan, the Kyrgyz Republic, the Republic of Moldovia, and the Republic of Armenia.

The African Regional Industrial Property Organization

The African Regional Industrial Property Organization (ARIPO), which was created by an agreement known as the Harare Protocol, grants patents that are recognized by and enforceable in its member countries. The member countries of the ARIPO are

Botswana	Mozambique	Swaziland
The Gambia	Namibia	Tanzania
Ghana	Sierra Leone	Uganda
Kenya	Somalia	Zambia
Lesotho	Sudan	Zimbabwe
Malawi		

The African Intellectual Property Organization

The African Intellectual Property Organization (OAPI) was created by an agreement known as the Bangui Agreement, and it grants patents that are recognized by and enforceable in its member countries. The member countries of the OAPI are

Benin	Côte d'Ivoire	Mali
Burkina Faso	Equatorial Guinea	Mauritania
Cameroon	Gabon	Niger
Central African Republic	Guinea	Senegal
Chad	Guinea-Bissau	Togo
Congo		

The Gulf Cooperation Council

The Gulf Cooperation Council likewise grants patents that are recognized by and enforceable in its member countries, which are Bahrain, Kuwait, Oman, Qatar, Saudi Arabia, and the United Arab Emirates.

Miscellaneous Treaties, Registration Provisions, and Automatic Extensions

Additional treaties exist, with a degree of overlap with the major treaties discussed above, but with the common goal of pooling resources to cover the administrative costs of patent examination and grant and of promoting unity and economic cooperation among member countries. One example is the Montevideo Treaty on Patents between Argentina, Bolivia, Paraguay, Peru, and Uruguay. This Treaty allows a patentee obtaining a patent in one country to obtain corresponding patent coverage in any other country within the Treaty by simply registering the first country patent in the other country within a year of the grant of the patent. A similar registration provision appears in the Caracas (Boliviariana) Convention, which extends to Bolivia, Colombia, Ecuador, Peru, and Venezuela. European patents that designate the United Kingdom can be registered in thirty-three additional countries and territories, the most notable of which is Hong Kong (where coverage can also be obtained by registering a patent granted in the People's Republic of China). U.K. patents themselves are enforceable in Botswana, Swaziland, and the British Indian Ocean Territory. As noted in Chapter 7, U.S. patents are enforceable in the territories and possessions of the United States as well as the states themselves. The territories and possessions are

American Samoa	Midway Atolls
Federated State of Micronesia	Midway Islands
Guam	Navassa Island
Guantanamo Bay	Palmyra Atoll
Howland, Baker, and Jarvis Islands	Palua
Johnston Island	Puerto Rico
Kingman Reef	Virgin Islands
Marshall Islands	Wake Island

The North American Free Trade Agreement (NAFTA) does not extend the enforceability of a patent beyond the borders of the country where the patent is granted, nor does it confer rights of priority. The Agreement does however have patent-related provisions relating to the type of proof that an inventor can offer to establish a date of invention. This is of value in situations where the date of invention determines the inventor's right to a patent.

The Agreement on Trade-Related Aspects of Intellectual Property Rights, Including Trade in Counterfeit Goods (commonly known as the "TRIPs Agreement"), which supersedes the earlier General Agreement on Tariffs and Trade (GATT), likewise does not extend the geographic scope of a patent or confer rights of priority, but obligates its approximately 150 member jurisdictions to harmonize certain provisions of their patent laws. The changes needed to meet these obligations must be enacted by the individual jurisdictions, however, and many are slow to do so.

COUNTRIES DENYING PATENTS ON DESIGNATED TYPES OF INVENTIONS

While countries throughout the world recognize the value of patents in promoting economic growth, the fact that a patent grants a monopoly to its owner has led many countries to refuse to grant patents in certain areas of technology where the interests of the patentee may conflict with what are perceived as national interests, fundamental human interests, or even moral standards. Since technology continually evolves, however, these views tend to change with time, and prohibitions against patenting are slowly receding. Nevertheless, an awareness of jurisdictions where prohibitions exist and the types of inventions that fall within these prohibitions are valuable to those who contemplate applying for patents on an international scale.

Pharmaceuticals and Medical Treatments and Diagnoses

The field of medicine is a sensitive area for patents in many jurisdictions, particularly for inventions that involve the sale or use of pharmaceuticals or clinical or surgical procedures that would benefit public health. The TRIPs Agreement obligates its member jurisdictions to grant patents for pharmaceuticals, but in many cases, revisions in the local patent laws to meet this obligation have not yet been made. In addition, many jurisdictions distinguish between the use of medical instruments in the diagnosis and treatment of diseases and the medical instruments themselves, by permitting patents on the instruments but not on their use. A novel instrument or device may thus be patentable whereas an invention defined in terms of a surgical, therapeutic, or diagnostic procedure involving the use of the instrument or device may not be patentable. Some of the more prominent jurisdictions (not a comprehensive list) where methods of treatment or diagnosis of humans and animals are not patentable are Canada, Mexico, the European Patent Office, China, Japan, Korea, Taiwan, Hong Kong, Singapore, Indonesia, Malaysia, and various South American countries. This is of particular concern where the invention resides in a new use of a known substance or device, such as the discovery that a chemical compound previously known only for nonmedical purposes can be used in a therapeutic or diagnostic procedure.

Nevertheless, in many of these jurisdictions, inventions for which patents are otherwise prohibited can avoid the prohibition by the use of specialized claim wording. In others, the local patent authorities are gradually liberalizing their approach. In Japan, for example, a revision made in 2005 to the official patent examination guidelines established that a method relating to the operation of a medical instrument was allowable while a method stated in terms of treating or diagnosing a human body with the same medical instrument was not allowable. The official example used to explain the distinction was an X-ray CT scanner, citing as allowable inventions: (1) the generation of an X-ray by controlling the X-ray–generating means in the scanner and (2) the detection of X-rays permeated through a human body by controlling the X-ray–detection component in the scanner, as opposed to inventions that included the step of irradiating the human body or of detecting X-rays permeating through the human body, both of which were cited as nonallowable. In terms of pharmaceuticals, inventions expressed in terms of a dosage form, a dose, an administration interval, a particular disease, particular patient conditions, and combinations of particular compounds are considered allowable, while inventions based on the discovery or use of a particular pharmacological property in a compound or combination of compounds are not allowable. This demonstrates the fine, and in some ways barely discernable, distinction between allowable and nonallowable subject matter. A greater advance occurred in India in December 2004, where a long-standing prohibition on patents to pharmaceuticals was removed entirely.

The law in Japan and similar laws in other countries present an interesting contrast with the patent laws of the United States, where a similar although more limited result is achieved by different means. The United States does not prohibit patents on pharmaceuticals or on therapeutic or diagnostic methods, but instead denies remedies to patent holders against medical practitioners for performing medical or surgical procedures on human bodies where the invention resides in the procedure. If however a medical instrument or device is itself patented, a practitioner using the device in a medical procedure is indeed liable to the patent holder. Patented pharmaceuticals are treated in the same manner as patented compositions of matter in general, with no restriction on the remedies available to the patent holder.

Computer Programs

Computer programs are frequently considered in the same light as mental processes, laws of science, and mathematical relations or algorithms in many jurisdictions and hence unpatentable, although liberalization has occurred in this area as well. Jurisdictions where computer programs are (or have been) expressly excluded from patentable subject matter include (again, not a comprehensive list) Canada, Mexico, the European Patent Office, Hong Kong, Singapore, the Russian Federation, and various South American countries. The United States, by contrast, does grant patents on computer programs.

Business Methods

Business methods are another manifestation of mental processes, but go well beyond to encompass a wide variety of business-related activities such as accounting methods, marketing methods, sales methods, inventory control methods, and the like. Prior to 1998, the United States categorically refused to grant patents on inventions that were deemed methods of doing business. This was changed by a decision of the U.S. Court of Appeals for the Federal Circuit in the case of *State Street Bank v. Signature Financial Group*, 149 F.3d 1368 (Fed. Cir. 1998). The Federal Circuit decision removed the prohibition, and business methods that meet the general requirements of patentability are now freely patentable in the United States. Many foreign jurisdictions however continue to deny patents to business methods. These jurisdictions include Canada, Mexico, the European Patent Office, China, Hong Kong, Singapore, Malaysia, and various South American countries.

Miscellaneous

In a number of jurisdictions, plant and animal varieties are either denied patents or subject to specialized patent provisions. These jurisdictions include Mexico, the European Patent Office, Brazil, Chile, Colombia, China, Taiwan, Hong Kong, the Russian Federation, and Malaysia. India has included prohibitions in its patent laws against inventions that are agricultural and horticultural methods, as well as inventions related to atomic energy. Indonesia has included prohibitions against patents to food or drink products and processes. Again, however, the patent laws in most countries of the world are ever in a state of flux, either because of gradual compliances with obligations under the TRIPs Agreement or simply to reflect changing economic and political climates.

WORKING REQUIREMENTS AND COMPULSORY LICENSING

Even for those inventions that are not subject to restrictions on patenting, many countries are reluctant to allow patent holders to utilize the patent right to its extreme, i.e., to allow the patent holder to prevent any practice of the patented invention within the geographical scope of the patent. This reflects the paradox of a patent: while the universal purpose of patents is to advance technology, no patent actually forces its owner to promote the growth of local industry by introducing the invention. Instead, a patent only confers upon its owner the right to exclude others from practicing the invention. Historically, a patent advanced the state of the art by its public disclosure of an invention in sufficient detail that others with a common level of skill in the relevant area of technology would be able to practice the invention from the information contained in the patent alone. As worldwide access to patents and published patent applications increased, however, to the point where patents and published applications are readily accessible virtually anywhere in the world, the need for a patent in one's own country for general information purposes is no longer present. This paradox is most apparent in countries outside the United States that have smaller economic and industrial bases and fewer technological resources. To address the need for patents to advance the state of technology rather than to restrict economic development, the patent laws of many of these countries include "working" requirements and provisions for "compulsory licenses."

A "working" requirement is generally a requirement that the patented invention be introduced into the country in some physical form rather than merely through the description in the patent. "Compulsory licensing" is an action by the patent authorities of a particular country forcing the patent owner to grant a nonexclusive license to a third party on terms imposed by the authorities. Compulsory licensing arises either from a failure of the patent owner to satisfy a working requirement, from a perceived economic necessity to the country, or from an abuse of the patent by the patent owner in a manner that causes damage to the economy of the country. Working requirements and compulsory licensing exist as complementary features of the law in many countries, but not all. Certain countries provide for compulsory licensing without a working requirement, and some provide for neither. Some of the more prominent countries that have neither are Canada, China, Japan, South Korea, and Taiwan.

In countries that impose a working requirement, the typical requirement is considerably less onerous than the term itself may suggest, since the requirement can often be satisfied by means other than actual working, and the consequences of a failure to satisfy the requirement are often remote. In fact, a review of the requirements in various countries reveals that the patent owner is generally allowed considerable latitude in satisfying the requirement. This latitude includes a grace period before working must be established, as well as certain options for satisfying the requirement other than actually practicing the patented technology within the country itself. With rare exceptions, the grace period is three years from the grant of the patent, or in some cases, three years from grant or four years from filing, whichever is later. In some other cases, however, working that has begun but is later suspended must be resumed within one year to prevent the patent from being subject to consequences for nonworking.

As for means other than actual working, certain countries accept the importation of a patented product or of a product of a patented process into the country as satisfaction of the working requirement. Countries that recognize importation as working are Mexico, the United Kingdom, Argentina, Brazil, the Andean Community countries (Colombia, Ecuador, Peru, Bolivia, and Venezuela), and Australia. Countries that do not are Hong Kong, Singapore, India, and New Zealand.

Still further countries accept working in other countries as satisfaction of the requirement in their own country. This is true in the Andean Community countries, where industrial manufacture of a patented product within the territory of any Community country will satisfy the working requirement in any other Community country, provided that the manufacture and distribution of the product is sufficient to meet market demands throughout the Community. In France, the working requirement can be satisfied by working of the invention in any member state of the European

Economic Community. In Germany, working can be satisfied simply by obtaining a corresponding patent in the United States.

In most countries, the issue of whether a working requirement has been satisfied is raised only by a party challenging the validity of the patent or seeking a compulsory license. The lone exception is India, where the patent owner is required to submit a written report to the patent authority every year stating whether working in India has occurred within the past year. A negative report can present an advantage to the aspiring compulsory licensee, although, as will be seen below, additional facts must be established before a license will be granted.

If the working requirement in any given country is not satisfied, the typical consequence is a susceptibility of the patent to compulsory licensing. In no country will a patent be nullified strictly for failure to meet a working requirement, although nullification is theoretically possible in certain countries if a compulsory license is granted and working has still not occurred, either by the patentee or the licensee, after a period of time, typically two years, from the grant of the license. Nevertheless, compulsory licenses arising from a failure to satisfy a working requirement are typically granted only to those who meet rather stringent requirements, and in many cases only after negotiations with the patent owner have failed. Compulsory licenses arising from abuse of the patent by the patent owner often lack a statutory basis but instead are granted by courts of law for equitable reasons after a persuasive showing of the nature of the abuse. These equitable reasons are typically based on whether terms asserted, or behavior engaged in, by the patentee are "reasonable" or "fair," which is generally decided on a case-by-case basis.

While compulsory licensing is a rare occurrence in most countries, a patent that is susceptible to compulsory licensing is generally less valuable than one that is not, since compulsory licensing limits the exclusivity enjoyed by the patent owner. A familiarity with the situations in which individual countries provide for compulsory licenses and with the requirements and limitations that they impose on the grant of these licenses may therefore be useful. Compulsory licensing provisions can, for example, provide insights into the use and enforceability of patents in these countries. Compulsory licenses also require that the patent owner confront its competitors, and hence the possibility of such a license can be a factor in various kinds of negotiations that involve intellectual property.

Illustration: Compulsory Licensing
in the United Kingdom

The compulsory license provisions in the patent law of the United Kingdom are an illustration of the different circumstances in which compulsory licenses can be granted. Familiarity with these provisions is instructive for those applying for patents in countries other than their own because most other countries of the world, particularly those that are members of the World Trade Organization (WTO), have some if not all of the same provisions, or provisions that are highly similar, in their patent laws.

Since the United Kingdom is a member of the WTO, compulsory licensing provisions in the United Kingdom offer a certain deference to other member countries of the WTO by making patents owned by WTO entities less susceptible to compulsory licenses. Thus, patents that are owned by persons or entities that are domiciles of a WTO country or have a "real and effective industrial or commercial establishment in a WTO country" are subject to compulsory licenses under fewer scenarios (and therefore offer greater exclusivity) than patents owned by those who are not domiciles of a WTO country. The various scenarios, and how they apply to WTO-owned patents versus non-WTO-owned patents, are as follows:

Licenses for Lack of "Working"

Like most other countries, the United Kingdom allows a grace period of three years from grant before a lack of working can be used as a basis for a compulsory license. Only product patents are susceptible to compulsory licenses for nonworking, and one area in which the law distinguishes between WTO-owned and non-WTO-owned patents is the degree to which working can be satisfied by importation. For WTO-owned patents, "working" can be satisfied by importation of the product into the United Kingdom from anywhere in the world. For non-WTO-owned patents, only importation from a member country of the EEA (European Economic Area) will constitute working. In both cases, the party seeking a compulsory license must show that there is a demand for the product in the United Kingdom that is not being met and that the patent owner refuses to license the patent on "reasonable grounds." These two requirements place a significant burden on the aspiring licensee. A second distinction between WTO-owned and non-WTO-owned patents is that for non-WTO-owned patents the "product demand" and "reasonable grounds" requirements are omitted entirely when the product is imported from outside the EEA. The only requirement for a compulsory license under these patents is that the patented invention be *capable* of being commercially worked (by means other than importation) in the United Kingdom and is *prevented* from being so by the importation.

Licenses under Dominating Patents

For both WTO-owned and non-WTO-owned patents, an improvement-type invention may provoke a compulsory license under a dominating predecessor patent. To qualify for the license, the owner of the improvement patent must show that a license under the dominating patent is needed if one wishes to practice the improvement, and that the improvement is "an important technical advance of considerable economic significance" relative to the dominating patent. While the necessary-to-practice requirement is relatively easy to meet or to assess, the requirements that the technical advance be "important" and that the economic significance be "considerable" are generally more difficult due to their lack of interpretive precision. Even if all requirements are met and the license is granted, the licensee must then be willing to allow the owner of the dominating patent a cross-license under the improvement patent.

Licenses to Inventions Needed for the Establishment or Development of Commercial or Industrial Activities

This provision likewise applies to both WTO-owned and non-WTO-owned patents, and is invocable only for commercial or industrial activities for which there is a specific need in the United Kingdom. While this provision may appear to be a rather liberal basis for granting a compulsory license, the aspiring licensee must establish not only that there is such a need but also that the commercial or industrial activities in question are "unfairly prejudiced" if licenses under the patent are withheld or if the license terms proposed by the patent owner are unreasonable.

Patents That Are Already Licensed But Affect
Materials, Commerce, or Industry That
Are Outside the Scope of the Patents

This provision, which likewise applies to both WTO-owned and non-WTO-owned patents, addresses licenses that carry conditions that affect the price or availability of materials that are not themselves covered by the licensed patent, or conditions that affect commercial or industrial activities in general. These scenarios are analogous to illegal or quasi-legal tying arrangements involving patents. The party that seeks a compulsory license on either of these grounds must show that commerce in the United Kingdom with respect to the materials, or the establishment or development of the industrial activities in question, are "unfairly prejudiced" by the conditions in the existing license.

Patents Affecting the Export Market

This ground for a compulsory license applies to non-WTO-owned patents only and to patents on inventions that affect the U.K. export market. When an export market for a particular product is not being supplied because of the refusal of a patent owner to either practice the patented invention or grant a license under the patent for export purposes, a compulsory license can be granted.

Patents on Semiconductor-related Inventions

The United Kingdom joins a number of other countries in favoring patents on semiconductor technology by adding further limitations to compulsory licenses on these patents. These limitations state that a compulsory license will not be granted under a semiconductor patent unless such a license is needed for a public noncommercial use or if the patent owner is using the patent in an anticompetitive way. This applies to both WTO-owned patents and non-WTO-owned patents. The semiconductor exclusion is a provision of the TRIPs Agreement referenced above, although not all TRIPs countries have implemented this provision. Countries in addition to the United Kingdom that have implemented this provision are South Korea, Taiwan, and India.

Miscellaneous Grounds

Although "national emergency" is not explicitly set forth under the U.K. patent law as a ground for a compulsory license, a number of countries do provide for compulsory licenses on this or similar grounds, using phrases such as "extraordinary state of affairs" or "particularly necessary for the public interest." Among these countries are Chile, China, Japan, South Korea, Taiwan, the Russian Federation, France, Germany, Denmark, Finland, and African countries that are signatories to the OAPI. Singapore provides for compulsory licensing any time after the grant of a patent for inventions that relate to food or medicine, or to surgical or curative devices.

Licenses of Right

The opposite of compulsory licensing is the patent owner that does not have a licensee and either wishes to have one or is receptive to any party seeking a license. Certain countries utilize the concept of a "license of right" to encourage patent owners, in exchange for certain benefits, to introduce the patented technology to the local industry by making a public offer to license the patent. The offer is made through the local patent authorities and published in an official patent gazette. Licenses offered in this manner are nonexclusive and royalty-bearing to the patent owner at rates determined by the patent authorities. The patent owner benefits by not having to otherwise satisfy the working requirement, and by being entitled to reduced annuities, which are the annual fees that the patent owner is obligated to pay to keep the patent in force. The reduction is typically 50%. The notice can be revoked by the patent owner at any time. Among the countries that provide for licenses of right with these benefits are the United Kingdom, France, Germany, Spain, Italy, New Zealand, Greece, Brazil, Singapore, and OAPI countries.

The term "license of right" is also used in some cases to designate licenses claimed by the local government for reasons relating to a national need for the use of the invention. Although government-claimed licenses are likewise royalty-bearing to the patent owner, these licenses are unrelated to the licenses of right that are offered by the patentee to the local industry at large.

Chapter 10

Inventors, Joint Inventors, and Unwilling Inventors

Patents are powerful tools of competition, and competition can arise not only from competitors but also from employees, collaborators, vendors, and independent contractors, in matters of inventorship, ownership, or both. When any of these matters come into question, the result can affect the company's right to practice the invention as well as its exclusivity and its ability to keep competitors from eroding its market position.

INVENTORSHIP

Sole Inventors versus Joint Inventors

The naming of inventors in a patent is a legal requirement in all patent jurisdictions throughout the world, even though the role that the inventor is required to play in the patenting process may vary among different jurisdictions. Most jurisdictions allow employers to apply for patents on their employees' inventions without the involvement of the employee in the patenting process, provided that the employee is obligated in some manner to transfer ownership of the employee's inventions to the employer. The United States has traditionally been the exception, requiring that the inventor(s) execute the application papers and, once the patent issues, granting ownership to the inventor(s) unless the inventor(s) has expressly assigned the application or patent to another, e.g., the employer of the inventor(s). U.S. patent law requires that all inventors be listed on a patent, and the consequence of an improper naming of inventors, whether by naming an individual who is not an inventor in place of one who is, or by providing an incomplete list of inventors, is an invalid patent. Improper inventorship has other consequences as well, and these may be of greater sensitivity to the inventors and their assignees. These range from resentment on the part of the omitted individual to issues of ownership of the patent and the right to practice the invention when different individuals either act independently or are under obligations to different employers.

Even though the patent statute requires the correct listing of inventors, the statute neglects to define an act of invention or to set forth the qualifications of an inventor. For joint inventors, the statute does little more than list items that *do not disqualify* one from joint inventorship status. The language appears in Section 116 of the statute and reads as follows:

> Inventors may apply for a patent jointly even though (1) they did not physically work together or at the same time, (2) each did not make the same type of contribution or amount of contribution, or (3) each did not make a contribution to the subject matter of every claim of the patent.

While this language fails to define the type of contribution that would qualify one as a joint inventor, one requirement that is generally accepted is that some form of collaboration among individuals is necessary if the individuals are to qualify as joint inventors. The clearest cases are easy to identify: (1) inventor A develops a partial solution to a problem and informs inventor B of A's findings without publicly disclosing them; inventor B then uses the unpublished findings to develop a complete solution and perfect the invention, with or without the assistance of A; versus (2) A publishes the partial solution without personally contacting B; B then uses the published information to develop the complete solution without the involvement of A. With the invention in both scenarios residing in the complete solution, A and B are joint inventors in the former scenario in view of their collaboration while B is the sole inventor in the latter due to the lack of collaboration. Most disputed cases are less clear, however, and questions of joint inventorship are often some of the most difficult to resolve in patent law. For the typical invention that resides in finding the solution to a problem, the critical act defining inventorship is generally held to be the conception of the solution, i.e., the conception of the means by which the desired result will be obtained, and all those contributing to this conception are joint inventors. The phrase "conception is the touchstone of invention" is thus used by both the courts and legal commentators. While the individual who actually contributes to the conception is readily distinguishable from the individual who simply suggests a desired result or does little more than follow the instructions of another, difficulties arise when the facts fall along the spectrum between these two extremes or when there is disagreement as to where along the spectrum the facts actually reside.

The point of division is indeed difficult to identify, but certain guidelines have been expressed by judicial authorities, notably the U.S. Court of Appeals for the Federal Circuit. Like the statute, the Court's position may be most clear in the negative, i.e., in its listing of those who are *not* joint inventors:

(1) Those whose involvement was limited to following the instructions or directions of others, performing routine tests, or compiling test results and conveying them to the others;

(2) Those whose sole contribution was to inform or educate the others as to previously existing methods or technologies that might affect the manner in which the invention was implemented or expressed;

(3) Those who originally identified the problem and/or proposed that a solution be sought without suggesting the solution that ultimately became the invention (an exception is where the discovery of the problem itself is part of the solution of a larger or related problem, and particularly where the solution is obvious once the problem is identified—whereupon the individual discovering the problem is a joint inventor); and

(4) Those who merely informed the others of the value of the invention or its potential.

Changes in Inventorship with Changes in the Invention

It is important to recognize that the feature of an invention that is asserted as the point of novelty of the invention, or the combination of features when the novelty lies in a combination, or the number of features when two or more features are set forth as independent points of novelty, may change between the time that the patent is first applied for and its date of issue. The change may arise from a modification of the patenting strategy to adapt to newly discovered "prior art" or to respond to other objections raised by a patent examiner. The change may also arise from a division of the patent application into two or more "divisional" patent applications, a common occurrence with inventions that are of broad scope or multifaceted. This change may require an amendment to the claims, either by reducing the scope of the broadest claim or by eliminating one or more claims in favor of the remaining claims. Amendments of this type may result in a change of inventorship, even if the original inventorship listing was correct when the application was filed. Such a change is a reflection of Section 116 of the statute, quoted above, which states that a contribution to the subject matter of any one claim in a patent qualifies the contributor as a joint inventor. Accordingly, the cancellation or addition of a claim may entail a loss or an addition, respectively, of inventorship status.

Rights of Joint Inventors

When joint inventors do exist, each inventor, in the absence of any agreement with the other inventors, has an undivided part interest in the patent, i.e., the ownership of the entire patent is divided equally among all joint inventors. This means that to the extent that there are no dominating patents or other obstacles to the inventors' rights to practice the invention, each joint inventor has the right to practice the invention without compensating or obtaining the consent of the other joint inventors. This right extends to all activities defined by the statute as infringing activities, i.e., making, using, selling, and offering to sell the invention within the United States, as well as importing the invention into the United States. A joint inventor's undivided right, however, does not include the right to claim a share in royalty revenues received by other joint inventors. Each joint inventor thus has the full right to assign or license his or her rights without sharing revenues with, or providing an accounting to, the other joint inventors.

ASSIGNMENT OF PATENT RIGHTS

Absent agreements to the contrary, patent rights are fully transferable, either by assignment or by exclusive or nonexclusive license. An assignment is a complete transfer of ownership of the entire patent and all rights that the patent entails, including the right to reassign the patent. A license is not a transfer of ownership, but it can still cover all of the rights under the patent. Alternatively, a license can be limited to some, but less than all, rights under the patent. A license cannot be granted on individual claims of the patent to the exclusion of others, since there is always a broad overlap among different claims of the patent. A license can however be restricted to a specified geographical area, a specified product or area of application, a specified time frame, or any specified portion or segment of the full rights under the patent. It is essential, however, that the licensor possess the right to grant the license. The assignee of the patent can thus grant any kind of license unless the assignment expressly forbids it, and a licensee can sublicense rights covered by its own license.

Disputes often arise when an employed inventor refuses to assign a patent to the inventor's employer or to otherwise cooperate with the employer in securing the employer's patent rights to the employee's invention. A refusal to disclose the invention to the employer or a refusal to provide the employer with test data needed to establish the utility of the invention or the improvement that the invention provides, particularly when such data are needed to support the patent, can prevent the employer from obtaining a patent. The most common disputes between employer and employee are over the employee's obligation to assign. Such a dispute may arise when the employment is terminated, either by employer or by employee, and the former employee obtains a patent and asserts it over the former employer, or when the employer applies for a patent without the involvement of the employee and circumvents the need for the employee's signature on the execution papers, including the assignment, by citing the employee's refusal to sign. Claiming rights from an employee who refuses to sign can be justified by a variety of reasons.

Contractual Obligations to Assign

An express obligation to assign patent rights is standard in most employment agreements. The typical clause reciting the obligation reads, at least in part, as follows:

> EMPLOYEE agrees to promptly disclose to EMPLOYER all inventions, improvements, and discoveries that EMPLOYEE has made or may make during EMPLOYEE's term of employment with EMPLOYER, that pertain

to or relate to the business of EMPLOYER or to any experimental work engaged in by EMPLOYER, regardless of whether EMPLOYEE conceives of such inventions, improvements, or discoveries alone or with others and of whether or not such inventions, improvements, or discoveries are conceived during working hours. EMPLOYEE agrees that all such inventions, improvements, and discoveries shall be the exclusive property of EMPLOYER, and agrees to assist EMPLOYER in obtaining patents on any such inventions, improvements, or discoveries that EMPLOYER deems to be patentable, by cooperating fully with EMPLOYER in supplying all information necessary in obtaining such patents, and by executing all documents necessary in obtaining such patents and in transferring ownership of such patents to EMPLOYER.

While this clause obligates the employee to cooperate with the employer in the preparation of the patent application and to sign the execution papers, which include a declaration (a required part of a patent application) and an assignment to the employer, the inclusion of the clause in the employment agreement does not make the agreement itself an assignment. The clause is merely an agreement to assign patent rights when they come into existence, whether they be an actual right, i.e., an issued patent, or an inchoate right, i.e., a pending patent application or an application that is fully prepared and ready to be filed. An employee's refusal to assign can simply be an employee's refusal to honor this obligation, or a disagreement between employee and employer as to when the invention was "made," i.e., conceived or completed, depending on which interpretation benefits which party.

The law does not generally look with favor upon agreements to assign rights in inventions that have not yet been made, since such agreements address property rights that have not yet come into existence. The law also recognizes that the employee is typically not in a position to negotiate an invention clause with the employer when the employment agreement is signed. For these reasons, the employee is typically given the benefit of the doubt when a clause of this kind becomes the subject of a lawsuit and is found to be open to interpretation. Even where the clause is explicit, it can be declared unenforceable if the obligation is deemed to be unreasonable, such as by lacking a time limitation after termination of employment.

In addition, a number of states have passed laws that benefit the employee by limiting the reach of these clauses. These states include California, Delaware, Illinois, Kansas, Minnesota, North

Carolina, and Washington, each of which has a statutory provision with essentially identical language. The typical language is found in § 2870 of the California Labor Code:

> Any provision in an employment agreement which provides that an employee shall assign, or offer to assign, any of his or her rights in an invention to his or her employer shall not apply to an invention that the employee developed entirely on his or her own time without using the employer's equipment, supplies, facilities, or trade secret information except for those inventions that either: (1) relate at the time of conception or reduction to practice of the invention to the employer's business, or actual or demonstrably anticipated research or development of the employer; or (2) result from any work performed by the employee for the employer.

A similar but broader provision appears in the Utah Code:

> An employment agreement between an employee and his employer is not enforceable against the employee to the extent that the agreement requires the employee to assign or license, or to offer to assign or license, to the employer any right or intellectual property in or to an invention that is: (a) created by the employee entirely on his own time; and (b) not an employment invention.

The refusal of an inventor to assign a patent application will not prevent the application from meeting the statutory or regulatory requirements for a patent. As noted above, however, the requirements do include a declaration signed by all inventors, and the refusal of an inventor to execute a declaration must be addressed. U.S. patent law (35 U.S.C. § 118) permits the employer, or anyone "to whom the inventor has assigned, or agreed in writing to assign, the invention or who otherwise shows sufficient proprietary interest in the matter," to apply for a patent on the inventor's behalf, i.e., without the inventor's signature on the declaration. This does not however place ownership of the patent or patent application in the employer.

"Hired to Invent"

The mere fact of employment carries no inference that the employee is obligated to assign patent rights to the employer. This is true even if the invention was made in the course of or as a consequence of work that the employee was hired to do, and even if the invention was made with the tools, time, and facilities of the employer. Nevertheless, in the absence of an employment agreement with a patent assignment clause or of any other express agreement to assign, the employee may still be obligated to assign ownership of a patent to his or her employer. This occurs when the employee was "hired to invent" or when the obligation to assign can be implied from the circumstances under which the invention was made.

An employee who was "hired to invent" is one who was initially hired or later directed to solve a specific problem or to exercise his or her inventive faculties in a particular area of technology. "Hired to invent" is distinguished from general employment, i.e., the mere hiring of an employee or the directing of an employee to simply make improvements on the employer's existing technology. General employment does not entail an obligation to assign, but the distinction between "hired to invent" and general employment is a delicate one that is open to interpretation and argument, and individual cases have led to many decisions rendered by courts of law. In general, determinations that an obligation to assign is or is not present have turned on the specificity of the task that the employee was hired to perform, the circumstances under which the invention was made, and the general practice within the company regarding employee inventions. Some of the factors that have influenced these decisions, without necessarily being the sole basis for a particular decision, are as follows:

1. Whether it was a customary practice in the company for employees to assign their inventions to the company, and if so, whether the employee knew of and acquiesced in the practice

2. Whether the concept or initial idea behind the invention originated within the company, such as with the employee's supervisor

3. The closeness of the connection between the invention and the company's business

4. Who provided the funding for the patent application, i.e., the attorney fees and filing fee

5. How the employer reacted to the invention when the invention was originally proposed by the employee

Fiduciary Duties of Officers and Directors

Another basis for an obligation to assign one's patent without an express agreement to do so is the status of an inventor as an officer or director of a corporation and the fiduciary duty that accompanies such a position. As with all issues regarding obligations to assign patents, the rules of law regarding the fiduciary duties of officers and directors and the extent to which these duties apply to patents are matters of state law rather than federal law, and as such, holdings expressed in official decisions in one state are not binding on other states. Nevertheless, courts in more than one state have held that all officers and directors of a corporation owe a fiduciary duty to the corporation, and that duty includes assigning to the corporation patents on inventions that were developed while the officer or director was employed by the corporation and that are related to the corporation's business. Most of the applications of the rule have involved presidents and chief executive officers, but the rule is considered to apply to all officers and directors. Exceptions have been made where the officer did not receive a salary from the corporation and where the officer had very limited authority that did not involve day-to-day involvement in the running of the corporation. Nevertheless, the general rule has not been denied in any state.

The "Shop Right"

A shop right is not an ownership right but instead an employer's right to practice an employee's invention, regardless of whether the employee is obligated to transfer ownership of the invention to the employer. Shop rights arise in inventions that are developed with the use of an employer's resources, such as the employer's tools, machinery, materials, and time. A shop right is effectively a license to use the invention without having to pay royalties, and it typically arises as a defense to a patent infringement action by the employee or by the owner of the patent if other than the employee. The existence of a shop right does not prevent the employee or the patent owner from granting licenses under the patent to other parties, royalty-bearing or otherwise. Shop rights are not generally transferable, i.e., the holder of a shop right cannot assign the right or sublicense the right to others. Exceptions arise when the employer's company is sold and continued in its entirety or merged into another company, the shop right being passed as part of the sale or merger.

Shop rights most often arise in an employment relation, but they can arise in other contexts as well. The invention of an independent contractor, for example, can be subject to a shop right in the company hiring the contractor. An invention that was conceived by an individual prior to employment, even one conceived with the individual's own equipment or materials, can be subject to a shop right in a company that later employs the individual if the invention is perfected and reduced to practice with company resources and on company time. Many of the same considerations that apply to "hired to invent" determinations apply to shop right determinations as well, and situations that can justify a shop right may also qualify for a transfer of ownership under a "hired to invent" theory. The facts that will convince a court of law to grant a shop right however are generally simpler to establish, and a shop right may be sufficient for the company's needs.

Chapter 11

Interim Protection for Inventions: Nondisclosure Agreements and Provisional Patent Applications

The proprietary nature of patentable technology can be preserved in a variety of ways short of the patent application process. This is true for technology that is also protectable as a trade secret but more effectively by a patent, as well as technology for which patenting is the only effective protection. Interim measures for preserving proprietary character and potential patentability are frequently used when the decision of applying for patent protection with its attendant costs and time commitments has not yet been made, and when the decision has been made but the time available is insufficient for the preparation of a fully developed patent application, due to an imminent disclosure, publication, commercial transaction, or implementation. Two of the most commonly used interim measures are nondisclosure agreements and provisional patent applications. Each has its limitations, however, and a full understanding of each will minimize the risk of losing one's patent rights and of harboring a false sense of security from these documents.

NONDISCLOSURE AGREEMENTS

Nondisclosure Agreements, or more aptly named in some situations as Confidential Disclosure Agreements, are agreements to provide someone with, or to allow someone access to, confidential information, in exchange for a promise by the recipient of the information not to disclose the information to others or, when disclosure to others is needed to serve the purposes of the agreement, to limit such disclosure to members of a specified group. The agreement may also include a promise not to analyze the information or to determine its composition or construction, particularly when the "information" is a chemical or biological material or any prototype, device or construction whose details are not discernable by simple observation, or a promise not to use the information for any purpose other than the purpose for which it was disclosed. A Nondisclosure Agreement can appear as a single paragraph or section of a larger agreement, or as a document of its own, ranging in length from a single page to multiple pages. Nondisclosure Agreements are used in a variety of settings, including:

A preliminary information exchange between separate business entities for purposes of determining whether there is a mutual level of interest in a possible alliance or collaboration and of evaluating the viability of the subject matter, or between a technology company and a potential investor to allow the investor to evaluate the investment, without losing the confidential or trade-secret status of the information

A service agreement between the creator of a new product, innovation, or design and an outside vendor whom the creator has engaged for a service such as constructing a prototype, preparing a sample, developing a manufacturing method, providing a quote for the cost of production, or performing a market analysis

A service agreement between a product developer and an outside testing facility to obtain test data for evaluating the functionality of the product or its performance in comparison to products already on the market, or to detect any side effects or undesirable features

A clause in an employment agreement or an agreement rendered upon termination of employment

The types of information that can be the subject of a Nondisclosure Agreement are formulas, drawings, specifications, samples, specimens, cell lines, prototypes, computer programs, test data, marketing information, and, in general, anything that is considered by the original possessor of the information to be proprietary or that, if made publicly available, would reduce or eliminate a present or potential economic advantage held by the original possessor. Among the advantages of a Nondisclosure Agreement are the following:

A.) It establishes the discloser of the information as the originator of the information, at least as between the discloser and the recipient; it clarifies the relationship between the discloser and the recipient of the information; and it sets boundaries that distinguish confidential from nonconfidential information.

B.) It notifies the recipient of the information that the information is considered confidential by the discloser and, if the agreement is violated by the recipient, it renders the recipient liable for any loss suffered by the discloser as a result of the violation.

C.) It preserves patent rights by preventing the disclosure itself from becoming public or otherwise acquiring the status of prior art.

Nondisclosure Agreements are typically subject to certain limitations, most of which have been developed by the courts in deciding the reasonableness and hence the enforceability of particular agreements. The obligation to keep the disclosed information confidential, for example, must be of reasonable duration and not unlimited in time. A common clause that appears in many agreements is one that limits the obligation to a term of five years from the signing of the agreement or three years from the last disclosure made under the agreement, whichever occurs later. Agreements are also commonly limited as to subject matter and, depending on the parties and the industry to which the subject matter pertains, the enforceability of the agreement may be geographically or territorially limited as well. The typical agreement will also be subject to automatic termination, either in whole or in regard to specific items of information, upon the occurrence of certain actions of the discloser of the information, most commonly an anticipated or unanticipated publication or a disclosure of the same information to another party without the same confidentiality restrictions. The Agreement may also call for automatic termination upon events arising at no fault to either party, such as a third-party publication or disclosure or a discovery that the information was already in the public domain. Additional causes for early termination will often be agreed to by the parties themselves.

While Nondisclosure Agreements can be of considerable value, there are certain functions that these agreements do not serve, notably:

A.) Unless explicitly provided for in the agreement, the agreement does not grant or transfer intellectual property rights to the disclosed information, either by assignment, license, or any other form of conveyance.

B.) Although the agreement will help preserve intellectual property rights, whether existing or potential, it does not itself create an intellectual property right.

C.) When the disclosed information is of a type that is susceptible to patent protection, the agreement does not prevent certain activities of the disclosing party from becoming prior art that might prevent the information from being patentable. This is true even for activities that do not involve public dissemination of the information and are not in violation of the agreement. Thus, the use of an invention for commercial purposes even if performed under security measures, and the sale or offer for sale of products or services embodying the invention, all constitute prior art which, if performed or made more than one year before filing a patent application, will bar the grant of a patent on the application.

D.) Of further concern to patent rights, the agreement does not prevent those who are not parties to the agreement from engaging in the same types of activities as those listed in the preceding paragraph, notably commercial uses performed either openly or under security, sales or offers for sale made independently of the parties to the agreement and with or without their knowledge, and publications that describe the subject matter.

E.) Of still greater concern to patent rights, the agreement does not preserve these rights for either party to the agreement when an outside party files a patent application on the same invention, particularly if the outside party files first and the prevailing rule is to award priority to the first to file.

To preserve the proprietary nature of valuable information, therefore, Nondisclosure Agreements have their greatest value when they are intended to be temporary and are used as a preliminary step toward a trade-secret license, toward applying for a patent, or toward any action or legal instrument that will establish an intellectual property right, including one that can be transferred, either by assignment or license, to the recipient of the information. The risk of a loss of intellectual property rights due to intervening events over which the parties have no control increases with the passage of time. As a result, the value of this preliminary step is greatest when the time between it and a subsequent, more secure, action, such as the filing of a patent application, is short.

PROVISIONAL PATENT APPLICATIONS

A provisional patent application is a document filed in the United States Patent and Trademark Office by or on behalf of an inventor as an optional preliminary step toward applying for a patent. The document can be filed without the formal requirements, and without all of the required components, of a nonprovisional (utility) patent application. A provisional can be filed without claims, for example, and without a declaration by the inventor(s), and the filing fee for a provisional is considerably lower than the filing fee for a nonprovisional. A provisional can also be filed in a language other than English without requiring the subsequent filing of an English translation. Despite its fewer requirements and lower cost, a provisional application is entered on the official record at the USPTO and receives an official application number and filing date, and its filing date can serve as the effective filing date of a later-filed nonprovisional (utility) application if certain legal requirements are met. These requirements include (1) the filing of the nonprovisional application within one year of the filing of the provisional and, of particular importance, (2) the inclusion in the provisional of sufficient description to meet the "enablement" requirement (discussed below) for the invention claimed in the nonprovisional.

In some cases, the filing date benefit offers a further advantage since, although it is the date that is used for evaluating the novelty of the invention in the nonprovisional, it does not serve as the starting point for calculating the expiration date of the patent ultimately issuing on the nonprovisional. That starting point is the filing date of the nonprovisional itself. To take advantage of this dual filing date effect, attorneys representing inventors in certain technologies have adopted a practice of preparing a fully developed patent application and filing it initially as a provisional application to establish an early date for novelty purposes, then re-filing the application as a nonprovisional at the last opportunity within the one-year period to achieve a patent expiration date as far into the future as possible. Since the term of enforcement of the patent when issued is not changed by this practice but only shifted back by approximately a year, this practice is useful only when the patent is not expected to achieve its value as an enforceable property right until several years after the provisional is filed. This will be true in certain areas in the field of biotechnology, for example, and other fields where new products and methodologies are required to undergo years of testing before they can be commercialized. In technologies that are less regulated or require less screening, the predominant advantage of a provisional application will be its ability to be filed in an expedited manner at low cost.

Whatever the technology of the invention, a provisional application offers numerous advantages in general, even though the application is not reviewed by a patent examiner and does not mature into a patent. With its reduced requirements, a provisional application can often be prepared more quickly than the typical nonprovisional. The shorter preparation time can be of considerable value when there is a pressing need to secure an early filing date. This need may arise for inventions in highly competitive fields in which other researchers are known to be working and are likely to make the same or similar discoveries. An early filing date may also be needed where a public disclosure of the invention is imminent and a filing date that precedes the disclosure is needed to prevent the disclosure from qualifying as prior art. In addition, the absence of a requirement to include claims allows an inventor to prepare and file a provisional application without the use of an attorney and without developing a claiming strategy. A provisional application can thus provide an inchoate intellectual property right with an early filing date at minimal cost, while the one-year period within which the filing date benefit can be transferred to a corresponding nonprovisional application gives the applicant valuable time for further investigation and decision making. The time can be useful for seeking financing or exploring prospects for financing or licensing; for testing the invention for technical, manufacturing, or commercial viability; or, in general, for postponing the decision as to whether to seek patent coverage.

Provisional applications should be used with caution, however, since their relative ease and low cost of preparation and filing can lead to certain misapprehensions. For example, the filing of a provisional application is not a means of reducing the cost of applying for a patent. If patent protection is ultimately desired, the applicant must replace the provisional with a nonprovisional application at a filing fee that is the same regardless of whether a provisional was first filed. Two filing fees are therefore incurred, and the total exceeds that of the nonprovisional alone. Likewise, unless the provisional and nonprovisional are identical, the attorney fees will be incurred for the nonprovisional and the total attorney fees for both applications will be at least as high as they would have been for a single application.

Nor does the provisional application permit the inventor (or an investor in the invention) to delay all patent-filing decisions. The one-year time limit applies not only to the filing of a U.S. nonprovisional application, but also to foreign filing under the Paris Convention, and extensions of the time limit are not available either in the United States or abroad. The Paris Convention does not permit one to transfer the filing date of a nonprovisional application to applications in foreign jurisdictions if the nonprovisional itself claims the benefit of a provisional application that was filed more than one year before the foreign applications.

The third and often most damaging misapprehension is that the timely filing of a nonprovisional application within the one-year period following the filing of a provisional will automatically entitle the nonprovisional to the benefit of the earlier filing date of the provisional. Frequently overlooked is the requirement that the provisional application provide sufficient disclosure to "enable any person skilled in the art ... to make and use" the invention claimed in the nonprovisional. Failure to meet this "enablement" requirement for any claim of the nonprovisional results in the loss of the benefit of the provisional filing date for that claim. Hastily drafted provisionals are particularly susceptible to this failure.

The "enablement" requirement is a statutory requirement (Section 112, first paragraph, of Title 35 of the U.S. Code) and represents a complex body of law that, for any invention, tends to reflect the particular technology in which the invention arises. In its broadest terms, an "enabling" disclosure is one that describes how to make and use the invention in a manner commensurate with the scope of the claims, while a "nonenabling" disclosure is one that is more of a statement of the invention than a description of how to make and use it. Experienced patent attorneys are familiar with the manner in which the USPTO and the patent courts approach the "enablement" requirement and are likewise familiar with the type of disclosure and the number and types of representative examples that are needed to support a broad claim for any particular technology. Provisional applications that are either not prepared by an attorney or prepared in haste entail the risk of failing to "enable" one or more claims of the ultimate patent.

In many cases, the risk results from the fact that the nonprovisional application typically has the benefit of additional time for its preparation. Nonprovisionals therefore tend to be more thoroughly thought out than provisionals, and this often results in a broadening of the inventive concept and hence of the scope of the invention, or a more detailed explanation of one or more of its features. New implementations of the principles of the invention and new examples are often added, or examples may be introduced for the first time if none were included in the provisional. The added time may also allow thought to be given as to how the invention can be expressed in narrower terms as back-up positions in the event that the original expression is found to be unrealistically broad either in terms of technical viability or in its distinction over the prior art. Thus, even if the provisional properly "enables" an invention of a certain scope, the nonprovisional may include claims of either a broader or narrower scope that are not "enabled" by the provisional and hence do not have the benefit of the earlier filing date of the provisional. This may simply mean that different claims of a patent may have different levels of vulnerability to challenge, which is true of any well-drafted patent application. It may also mean however that the claims that the patent holder chooses to assert in an infringement action may be unenforceable due to their inability to benefit from an early filing date.

This was indeed the result in a published decision of the U.S. Court of Appeals for the Federal Circuit (*New Railhead Manufacturing LLC v. Vermeer Manufacturing Co.*, 63 USPQ 2d 1843 (2002)) in which Patent Nos. 5,899,283 and 5,950,743 were declared invalid due to commercial sales more than one year prior to the filing dates of the nonprovisional applications from which the patents were granted. The patents covered a mechanical device for trenchless drilling, and before any patent applications were filed, commercial sales of the devices were made. A provisional application was filed six months after the first commercial sales, and the two nonprovisionals were filed nine months after the provisional. Thus, if the nonprovisionals had been allowed the filing date benefit of the provisional, both nonprovisionals and hence the two patents would have fallen within the one-year grace period following a commercial sale, and would therefore have been upheld and enforced. The claims of both patents were expressly limited, however, to devices in which the drill bit was at a particular orientation relative to the sonde (a component that sends positioning data to a receiver above the ground surface), and the provisional failed to include mention of this orientation. As a result, neither patent was allowed the benefit of the filing date of the provisional, and both patents were declared invalid due to their filing dates falling outside the grace period after the commercial sales.

The provisional application in the *New Railhead Manufacturing* case had in fact been worded broadly enough to encompass drilling devices of any drill bit orientation; what was lacking was a reference to the particular orientation that was ultimately claimed in the two patents. This is an example of a provisional that is broad but lacking in description to flesh out its breadth, and accordingly lacking support for a narrowly defined feature that was later decided to be critical to patentability. Provisionals that fail for being too narrow, on the other hand, often arise in chemical and biotechnical inventions, where, for example, a provisional application may consist of little more than a description of one or more working examples as supplied by the inventor and only after the provisional has been filed is a generic formula or description devised. If the generic patent issues and the patent holder seeks to assert over an infringer a portion of the genus that lies outside the scope of the original working examples, the patent may not able to benefit from the filing date of the provisional. An intervening publication or use by the infringer or by any outside party may then invalidate claims to anything other than the original examples.

Filing provisional applications routinely is useful in technologies where the pipeline to commercialization is long and where there is a need for both an early filing date for novelty purposes and a late expiration date. Filing provisional applications on an individual basis rather than routinely is useful where an imminent event presents a potential loss of rights and therefore a pressing need for an early filing date. In either case, a provisional application is most effective when prepared by a patent attorney and when it includes as much description and thought as to different degrees of breadth as the available preparation time will allow. The closer the provisional is to a nonprovisional in terms of form and content, the greater its value. The greater the amount of description and the number of examples and drawings in the provisional, the less the risk that the claims of the nonprovisional will be denied the benefit of the filing date of the provisional and therefore vulnerable to challenge over intervening prior art.

Glossary

Abbreviated New Drug Application. An application to the Food and Drug Administration for marketing approval of a generic drug that, due to the generic nature of the drug, is not required to include preclinical and clinical data to establish safety and effectiveness.

Absolute novelty. The quality of an invention of not having been publicly disclosed prior to the submission of a patent application on the invention to a patent authority, a requirement for the grant of a patent in many jurisdictions outside the United States.

African Intellectual Property Organization. A regional patent authority covering sixteen countries in western Africa.

African Regional Industrial Property Organization. A regional patent authority covering sixteen countries in southern and eastern Africa.

ANDA. See Abbreviated New Drug Application.

Anticipation. A cause for rejection of a claim of a patent application, or for declaring a claim of a patent invalid, for reciting an invention that fails to possess novelty.

Appeal. A review procedure by an authority within the U.S. Patent and Trademark Office above the level of an examiner, initiated by a patent applicant dissatisfied with the decision of an examiner.

ARIPO. See African Regional Industrial Property Organization.

Assignee. A person or entity to which ownership of a patent or patent application has been transferred.

Assignment.   The transfer of ownership of a patent or patent application from one entity to another.

Assignor.   One who transfers ownership of a patent or patent application to another.

Claims.   Legal expressions of the scope of activity which a patent affords its owner the right to exclude others from practicing.

"Comprises" or "comprising."   Terms used in claim language to indicate that all elements following the term must be present in an accused article or activity to constitute infringement, and that the presence of additional elements will not remove the accused article or activity from infringement liability.

Compulsory licensing.   The granting of a license under a patent, regardless of the wishes of the patent holder although typically with compensation to the patent holder, by the government in a country where the patent is in force, for reasons related to the perceived needs of the country.

Conception.   The formation in the mind of an inventor of the idea that later becomes the invention claimed in a patent application.

Confidential disclosure agreement.   An agreement (also referred to as a "nondisclosure agreement") to convey information, generally for purposes of evaluation prior to entering into a strategic alliance, in exchange for a promise not to disclose the information to others.

"Consisting essentially of."   A term used in claim language to indicate that all elements following the term must be present in an accused article or activity to constitute infringement, and that the presence of one or more additional elements may remove the accused article or activity from infringement liability unless the additional elements are deemed insignificant in quantity or effect.

"Consisting of."   A term used in claim language to indicate that all elements following the term, and only those elements, must be present in an accused article or activity to constitute infringement, and that the presence of one or more additional elements will remove the accused article or activity from infringement liability.

Continuation application.   A patent application with a specification identical to that of an earlier-filed patent application and claiming certain filing date benefits of the earlier application, filed by the applicant to achieve certain procedural benefits before the USPTO.

Continuation-in-part application. A patent application with descriptive content in common with an earlier-filed patent application in addition to descriptive content not present in the earlier application, yet claiming certain filing date benefits of the earlier application, filed by the applicant to seek either broader or stronger coverage.

Contributory infringement. An activity falling short of infringement but still giving rise to liability under a patent.

Copyright. A work of authorship that is fixed in a tangible medium of expression.

Defensive publication. A document issued by the USPTO (discontinued after 1986) at the request of an applicant and disclosing an invention, but conferring no rights on the applicant and having no legal effect other than as prior art relative to later-filed patent applications.

Dependent claim. A claim that explicitly refers to another claim and thereby incorporates all limitations of the claim referred to.

Design patent. A patent directed to ornamental features of an article rather than utilitarian or functional features.

Direct infringement. The meeting of all limitations of at least one claim of a patent.

Divisional application. A patent application with a specification identical to that of an earlier-filed patent application and claiming certain filing date benefits of the earlier application, filed by the applicant to seek examination of claims that were set aside ("withdrawn from consideration") in the earlier application following a restriction requirement, i.e., a ruling by the examiner that different claims in the application would support different patent applications.

Doctrine of Equivalents. A legal doctrine by which an accused activity that meets less than all of the limitations of a claim is nevertheless deemed to infringe the claim if the distinction that brings the activity outside the claim is deemed to be insignificant.

Domain name. The text name corresponding to the numeric IP address of a computer on the Internet.

Dominating claim or patent. A claim, or a patent containing a claim, whose scope encompasses the scope of a claim of a later patent, with the result that operating within the scope of the latter will constitute infringement of the former.

Double patenting. The claiming by a single applicant of inventions in two patents or patent applications whereby the two inventions are deemed not to be patentable over each other.

Due diligence. A review preceding a transaction for the purpose of assessing the value of an asset being sold or an interest being acquired by the transaction and revealing any obstacles or mitigating factors.

EAPO. See Eurasian Patent Office.

Effective date. In connection with prior art, the date of an occurrence or document that determines whether that occurrence or document has the status of prior art against which the novelty of an invention is determined; in connection with a patent or patent application, the filing date attributed to that patent or application against which an occurrence or document is compared to determine whether the occurrence or document is prior art.

Enablement. The quality of a patent specification of describing the claimed invention in sufficient detail that the technically skilled reader can practice the invention from the description itself, a requirement of U.S. patent law.

EPO. See European Patent Office.

Eurasian Patent Office. A regional patent authority covering nine Eurasian countries.

European Patent Convention. A regional patent convention covering thirty-eight European countries.

European Patent Office. The patent office created under the European Patent Convention.

Exclusive license. A right granted to a party by a patent owner to engage in activity within the scope of a patent without being sued by the patent owner for infringement, coupled with an agreement by the patent owner not to grant such a right to others. A co-exclusive license is one in which the right is granted to two or more parties with mutual knowledge of the grants and an agreement by the patent owner not to grant to further parties.

Experimental use. An exception to certain business or commercial activities, transactions, or communications that would otherwise constitute prior art.

Expiration date. The date after which a patent is no longer enforceable for reasons other than having been declared unenforceable by a court of law.

Family. A collection of patents, patent applications, or both, often including those filed in different jurisdictions, that claim mutual filing date benefits.

Fiduciary duty. Any of various obligations of officers and directors of a corporation to the corporation, notably the rights to patentable inventions invented by the officer or director.

File history. The official record of a patent application on file at the USPTO.

Filing date, actual. The date on which a patent application is received by a patent authority, or the date recognized by the authority as that on which the application is received.

Foreign priority. The filing date benefit afforded under the Paris Convention to a patent application in one jurisdiction by a patent application filed less than one year before in another jurisdiction.

Freedom to operate. The ability to engage in commercial activity without incurring liability due to legal obstacles such as patent infringement and regulatory prohibitions.

GATT. See General Agreement on Tariffs and Trade.

GCC. See Gulf Cooperation Council.

General Agreement on Tariffs and Trade. A multinational agreement containing provisions for harmonizing patent laws.

Gulf Cooperation Council. A regional patent authority covering six Arab countries.

Hatch-Waxman Act. Full name: Drug Price Competition and Patent Term Restoration Act of 1984. A law that addresses and reconciles provisions of the patent law and the federal regulatory process for drugs, with the purposes of encouraging competition in the drug industry and reinforcing patent rights that would otherwise be eroded by the regulatory process.

Indemnity. A provision in a contract obligating one party to the contract to reimburse a second party for costs incurred in defending claims brought against the second party for performing acts pursuant to the contract.

Independent claim. A claim in a patent that is self-contained and does not refer to another claim.

Inducement to infringe. The active and knowing assistance to a person or entity in infringing a patent.

Infringement. The act of practicing an invention covered by a patent without permission from the patent owner.

INID. See Internationally Agreed Upon Numbers for the Identification of Bibliographic Data.

Intellectual property. Patents, copyrights, trademarks, trade secrets, and intangible assets in general that embody proprietary technology.

Interference. An administrative procedure before the USPTO to resolve conflicting claims of multiple parties to patent rights to a single invention.

International application. A patent application filed under the provisions of the Patent Cooperation Treaty (PCT).

International phase. The phase of an international application between its initial filing as an international application and its subsequent submission to regional patent authorities that are empowered to grant patents.

International Preliminary Examination Report. A statement issued by authorized officials under the PCT evaluating an international application in accordance with standards of patentability established under the Treaty.

Internationally Agreed Upon Numbers for the Identification of Bibliographic Data. A series of standardized indices used by patent jurisdictions as a guide to the identity of various pieces of information included on the cover pages of patents.

Inventor. One who supplies a creative contribution to the conception of an invention as expressed in at least one claim of a patent.

Issue date. The date on which the USPTO issues a patent on a patent application, and the start of the time period during which the patent owner can exercise the full rights of patent ownership.

Joint inventors. Two or more persons who collaborate on an invention by each making a creative contribution to the conception of the invention as expressed in at least one claim of a patent on the invention.

Joint venture. A type of strategic alliance in which two or more independent corporate entities combine resources for the development of a product, each entity retaining its own corporate identity.

License. In patents, an agreement between a patent owner and a second party by which the patent owner agrees to allow the second party to practice the invention covered by the patent without pursuing legal remedies against the second party for infringement.

License of right. In certain patent jurisdictions outside the United States, a public offer of licenses to an invention by the patent holder to satisfy a working requirement; also, a license claimed by the local government of a country to satisfy a national need for use of the invention.

Licensee. In patents, the party in a license to whom is transferred the right to practice the invention without being liable to the transferor for patent infringement.

Licensor. In patents, the party in a license who conveys the right to practice the invention without being liable to the conveying party for patent infringement.

Limitation. A descriptive element in a patent claim that must be met by an accused infringer before the infringer can be held liable for infringement of the claim.

Literal infringement. The act of meeting all limitations of at least one claim of a patent in the form in which the limitations are expressed in the claim.

"Means for" or "means plus function." A type of phrase used in claim language that includes the words "means for" followed by a gerund and is met by any structure, material, or acts set forth in the specification that perform the function expressed by the gerund, and any recognized equivalents of the structure, material, or acts.

National phase. In a PCT application, the phase (also known as the regional phase) after which the application has been forwarded to the patent authorities of individual countries or regions that are empowered to grant patents, where the application is examined under local standards; in a European application, the phase after which a patent granted on the application by the European Patent Office has been made enforceable ("validated") in individual countries that are members of the European Patent Convention.

Nonexclusive license. A right granted to a party by a patent owner that allows the party to engage in activity within the scope of a patent without being sued by the patent owner for infringement, while allowing the patent owner to grant the same right to others.

Nonobviousness. A fundamental requirement of patentability in U.S. patent law that refers to the degree or quality of difference between the invention and the prior art.

Nonprovisional application. A U.S. utility patent application that is eligible for examination toward issuance of a utility patent (also referred to as a "regular" patent application).

North American Free Trade Agreement. An agreement between the United States, Canada, and Mexico removing certain barriers to trade and investment between the three countries and including provisions regarding the type of evidence that an inventor domiciled in one country can offer in a second country to establish a date of invention when applying for a patent in the second country.

Novelty. A fundamental requirement of patentability in U.S. patent law that is satisfied by any distinction between the invention and the prior art.

OAPI. See African Intellectual Property Organization.

Obviousness. A cause for rejection of a claim in a patent application, by which the claimed invention, although satisfying the novelty requirement, is deemed not to be sufficiently different from the prior art to merit the issuance of a patent—the absence of nonobviousness.

Office action. An official written communication from an examiner at the USPTO to a patent applicant (or to the applicant's patent attorney or agent) setting forth the examiner's conclusion of whether or not the patent application meets the legal requirements (including novelty and nonobviousness) of a patent.

Paris Convention for the Protection of Industrial Property. A multinational agreement whose primary feature is the recognition of the filing date of a patent application in one country as the effective filing date for corresponding patent applications on the same invention and filed by the same inventor or assignee in other countries.

Patent. A legal instrument affording its owner the right to exclude others from engaging in activity within precisely delineated boundaries for a limited period of time and within a limited geographical area. When used alone in connection with U.S. patents, the term generally denotes a utility patent.

Patent agent. A person who, although not an attorney, is licensed by the USPTO to represent inventors before the USPTO in their efforts to obtain patents.

Patent attorney. An attorney licensed by a state bar to practice law and also licensed by the USPTO to represent inventors in their efforts to obtain patents.

Patent Cooperation Treaty. A multinational agreement whose purposes are to encourage harmonization of patent laws among its signatories and to allow patent applicants applying for patents in a multitude of countries to establish filing dates for all of the countries by filing the patent application in a single receiving office.

Patent of addition. In certain patent jurisdictions other than the United States, a patent of limited scope that is an adjunct to a utility patent and claims an improvement or modification of the invention in the utility patent.

"Patent pending." The stage at which a patent application has been filed with the USPTO and has neither matured into an issued patent nor been abandoned.

Patentability. The quality of an invention by which the invention meets the legal requirements for the issuance of a patent.

PCT. See Patent Cooperation Treaty.

Plant patent. A patent issued by the USPTO on certain types of living plants rather than on inventions or designs.

Pre-grant patent publication. A version of a patent application that is published by the USPTO approximately eighteen months after the earliest filing date from which the application claims benefit, and that affords the owner of the application certain provisional rights in addition to the rights under the patent itself if and when a patent issues on the application (also referred to as "pre-grant publication").

Prior art. A legal term referring to all forms of activity, including published and nonpublished matter, over which an invention must be shown to be both novel and nonobvious to qualify for a patent.

Priority document. Any patent application whose filing date is transferred to or shared with a subsequently filed patent application, either in the same jurisdiction or another jurisdiction, for purposes of establishing whether certain activity qualifies as prior art relative to the later application.

Provisional application. A document submitted to the USPTO as an optional preliminary step toward applying for a utility patent, and potentially serving as a priority document for the utility patent application.

Provisional right. The right of a patent owner to demand royalties for the practice of a patented invention during the period between the publication of the patent application (see Pre-grant patent publication) and the issuance of the patent.

PTO. United States Patent and Trademark Office.

Reduction to practice. The physical implementation of an invention, typically to confirm that the invention functions as conceived or that it can be constructed or otherwise made as conceived. In an interference, the filing of a patent application can serve as a "constructive reduction to practice" for purposes of establishing priority of invention despite a lack of a physical implementation of the invention prior to the filing.

Re-examination. The re-submission of a patent, despite having already been granted, to the USPTO either by the patent owner or a challenger of the patent, to address issues of patentability that were not addressed during the original examination that resulted in the grant of the patent.

Regional phase. In a PCT application, the phase (also known as the *national* phase) after which the application has been forwarded to the patent authorities of individual countries or regions that are empowered to grant patents, where the application is examined under local standards.

Reissue application. The re-submission of a patent, despite having already been granted, to the USPTO by the patent owner to seek a change in some aspect of the patent, on the ground that due to error the patent claims either more or less than the patent owner had the right to claim.

Related application. A patent application that claims a filing date benefit from another patent application.

Secrecy order. An order imposed by a branch of the U.S. military prohibiting public disclosure of the contents of a patent application and thus preventing a patent from issuing on the application for a specified period of time due to a potential interest in the subject matter of the application for national defense.

Service mark. A symbol such as a name, logo, or slogan that accompanies a service, associating the service with the supplier of the service such that those encountering the symbol in connection with another service will attribute both services to the same supplier.

Shop right. An employer's right to practice the invention of an employee without compensation to the employee, when the invention was developed with the use of the employer's resources, such as the employer's equipment, materials, and time.

Sole inventor. An individual who is the sole source of creative input to the conception of an idea that forms the basis for an invention.

Specification. The portion of a patent or patent application in which the invention and any associated prior art are described, i.e., the text of the patent or application exclusive of the title, abstract, claims, and drawings.

Statutory bar. An obstacle to the grant of a patent on an invention, due to a printed publication (including granted patents and pre-grant patent publications) describing the invention, or a sale or offer for sale of an embodiment of the invention, more than one year prior to the effective filing date of a patent application on the invention. See Swearing back.

Statutory invention registration. A document issued by the USPTO similar in appearance to, but lacking the enforceability of, a utility patent, and whose purpose is to place the information contained in the document in the public domain.

Strategic alliance. A joint agreement between two or more business entities to combine resources for the economic benefit of both, for example, to develop revenue from a patent portfolio.

Swearing back. Overcoming a rejection of, or challenge to, a patent application or patent due to prior art by providing evidence of a date of invention that precedes the effective date of the document or activity cited as prior art. Permitted under U.S. patent law except when a statutory bar is present.

Term of patent. The period of time during which the practice of the invention expressed in one or more claims of a patent constitutes infringement of the patent.

Terminal disclaimer. A forfeit by a patent applicant or patent holder of a portion of the term of a patent at the end of the term to cause the patent to expire on the same date as another, commonly owned (reference) patent, for purposes of removing the reference patent as prior art relative to the patent whose term has been shortened by the disclaimer.

Trade secret. Any information of commercial value to a business entity that is proprietary to the entity and maintained so by preventing public dissemination of the information.

Trademark. A symbol such as a name, logo, or slogan that accompanies goods, associating the goods with the supplier of the service such that those encountering the symbol in connection with other goods will attribute both goods to the same supplier.

Trade-Related Aspects of Intellectual Property Rights, Including Trade in Counterfeit Goods. A multinational agreement that establishes a framework of principles, rules, and disciplines dealing with intellectual property and its impact on international trade, including provisions for intellectual property rights, enforcement measures for those rights, and multilateral dispute settlement.

Transitional rule. A method of determining the expiration date of a U.S. utility patent that was either a pending application or an enforceable patent on June 8, 1995.

TRIPs Agreement. See Trade-Related Aspects of Intellectual Property Rights, Including Trade in Counterfeit Goods.

USPTO. United States Patent and Trademark Office.

Utility. A fundamental requirement of patentability in U.S. patent law that is satisfied by an invention that possesses a utilitarian function.

Utility model. A type of patent protection that is offered in certain jurisdictions outside the United States, with a term typically shorter than those of a conventional patent, and generally for inventions that lack sufficient differences over the prior art for full patent protection.

Utility patent. A U.S. patent that claims utilitarian features of an invention.

Validity of claim or patent. The quality of a single claim or of all claims in an unexpired patent by which the claim or patent meets all legal requirements for enforceability.

Warranty. An assurance by one party to a contract that a representation in the contract, such as the validity or enforceability of a patent or the freedom to practice an invention without liability to other patent holders, is truthful and that is relied upon by other parties to the contract as part of the exchange of obligations in the contract.

WIPO. See World Intellectual Property Organization.

Working requirement. A feature of patent laws in certain countries outside the United States obligating a patent holder to either initiate a commercial practice of the invention within the geographical jurisdiction of the patent or to make the invention available for licensing.

World Intellectual Property Organization. An organization implementing the provisions of the PCT.

Written Opinion. An official document issued by WIPO in connection with a PCT patent application, evaluating the invention in the application in reference to the standards set forth in the PCT.

References and Supplementary Materials

BOOKS

Anson, Weston, and Donna Suchy, eds., *Fundamentals of Intellectual Property Valuation—A Primer for Identifying and Determining Value*, Chicago: American Bar Association, Section of Intellectual Property Law (2005).

Aspelund, Donald J., et al., *Employee Noncompetition Law*, St. Paul, MN: West Group (2000).

Brunsvold, Brian G., *Drafting Patent License Agreements, Fourth Edition*, Washington, DC: BNA Books (1998).

Durham, Alan L., *Patent Law Essentials—A Concise Guide*, Westport, CT: Praeger Publishers (2004).

Finkelstein, William A., and James R. Sims III, *Intellectual Property Handbook: A Practical Guide for Franchise, Business and IP Counsel*, Chicago: American Bar Association, Section of Intellectual Property Law (2005).

Glazier, Stephen C., *Patent Strategies for Business*, 3rd ed., Washington, DC: LBI Institute (2000).

Hanellin, Elizabeth, ed., *Patents Throughout the World*, St. Paul, MN: West Group (2000).

Heines, M. Henry, *Patent Empowerment for Small Corporations*, Westport, CT: Quorum Books (2001).

Henn, Harry A., *Copyright Law—A Practitioner's Guide*, 2nd ed., New York: Practicing Law Institute (1988).

Hitchcock, David, *Patent Searching Made Easy*, Berkeley: Nolo Press (1999).

Keller, Bruce P., et al., *Conducting Intellectual Property Audits*, New York: Practicing Law Institute (1995).

Lechter, Michael A., ed., *Successful Patents and Patenting for Engineers and Scientists*, New York: The Institute of Electrical and Electronics Engineers, Inc. (1995).

Malsberger, Brian M., *Employee Duty of Loyalty: State-by-State Survey, Third Edition*, Chicago: American Bar Association, Section of Intellectual Property Law (2005).

Pedowitz, Arnold H., et al., *Trade Secrets—A State-by-State Survey*, Washington, DC: Bureau of National Affairs, Inc. (1997) and supplements.

Pienkos, John T., *The Patent Guidebook*, Chicago: American Bar Association, Section of Intellectual Property Law (2004).

Rivette, Kevin G., and David Kline, *Rembrandts in the Attic*, Cambridge, MA: Harvard Business School Press (2000).

Seidel, Arthur H., et al., *What the Practitioner Should Know about Patent Law and Practice*, 6th ed., Philadelphia: American Law Institute—American Bar Association Committee on Continuing Professional Education (1998).

Smith, Gordon V., et al., *Valuation of Intellectual Property and Tangible Assets*, 2nd ed., New York: John Wiley & Sons (1994).

Stobbs, Gregory A., *Business Method Patents*, New York: Aspen Law & Business (2002).

WEB SITES

American Bar Association Section of Intellectual Property: www.abanet.org

Canadian Patent Office: www.cipo.gc.ca

Intellectual Property India: www.patentoffice.nic.in

The Intellectual Property Owners Association: www.ipo.org

Japanese Patent Office: www.jpo.go.jp

The Licensing Executives Society International: www.lesi.org

Mexican Patent Office: www.impi.gob.mx

The National Association of Patent Practitioners: www.napp.org

State Intellectual Property Office of the Peoples Republic of China: www.sipo.gov.cn

United States Copyright Office: www.copyright.gov

United States Patent and Trademark Office: www.uspto.org

World Intellectual Property Office (Patent Cooperation Treaty): www.wipo.int

Index

About the Author

M. HENRY HEINES is a chemical engineer, patent attorney, and partner in the law firm of Townsend and Townsend and Crew LLP, headquartered in San Francisco. He has over 30 years of experience advising large and small businesses, universities, research institutions, and venture capitalists in such fields as chemistry, biotech, semiconductors, medical devices, and laboratory instruments. He is the author of many articles on the management of patents, and serves as Patent Editor of *Chemical Engineering Progress*. He is also the author of *Patent Empowerment for Small Corporations* (Quorum, 2001).